Contents

Registration Regulations

Fees & Frequency of Inspections Regulations

National Minimum Standards

Abbreviations:

CA 1989 = Children Act 1989

CAFCASS = Children & Families Courts Advisory & Support Service

CRB = Criminal Records Bureau

CSA 2000 = Care Standards Act 2000

NCSC = National Care Standards Commission

PA 1997 = Police Act 1997

POCA 1999 = Protection of Children Act 1999

Introduction

This guide is designed for use in England, by those who provide or work in, fostering services and agencies.

It is intended to facilitate understanding of the obligations and expectations of the Care Standards Act 2000 (CSA 2000), Children Act 1989 (CA 1989), other relevant regulations and the national minimum standards.

The CSA 2000 created the National Care Standards Commission (NCSC), an independent non-departmental body responsible for regulation of a range of health and care services, including foster care of children.

The NCSC assesses, on the basis of the Fostering Services Regulations 2002 (compliance with which is mandatory), and achievement of national minimum standards (issued by the Secretary of State under s.23 (1) CSA 2000), whether services being provided by a local authority, an independent fostering agency or a voluntary organisation are satisfactory.

When the NCSC makes any decision about registration, cancellation, variation or imposition of conditions, it must take the national minimum standards as well as any other factors considered reasonable and relevant into account.

With respect to independent fostering agencies and voluntary organizations, if a regulation is breached and an offence committed, providers will be given a notice setting out:

- Regulation breached
- How the service is considered deficient

- What must be done to remedy the deficiency
- A time-scale within which the deficiency must be remedied

If the deficiency is not remedied, a prosecution may follow.

In the case of a local authority service, the enforcement route is via the Secretary of State to whom the NCSC will report a substantial failure to meet a regulation. If there is a failure which is not substantial, the NCSC may serve an enforcement notice under s.47 (5) CSA 2000.

The UK National Standards for Foster Care, produced in 1999, along with the Code of Practice on the recruitment, assessment, approval, training, management and support of foster carers, remain applicable to fostering services.

They cover all aspects of the life of a fostered child, and although they have no formal legal status, they represent best practice and should be fully complied with by fostering service providers.

With effect from April 1 2004, the newly created Commission for Social Care Inspection (CSCI) is scheduled to cover all the work of the Social Services Inspectorate, the joint review team of the SSI / Audit Commission and the functions of the National Care Standards Commission.

NB. We have generally used the more popular term 'foster carer' except in our summary of regulations where the term 'foster parent' is used to reflect the term used in primary and subordinate legislation.

Definitions (in alphabetical order)

Child

- A person aged less than 18 years old.

Fostering Service [Reg.2 Fostering Services Regulations 2002]

- A fostering service means:
  - A fostering agency as defined in s.4(4) CSA 2000 i.e. a private or voluntary organisation that carries out fostering functions of a local authority or
  - A local authority fostering service
- An 'independent fostering agency' is one falling within the definition of s.4(4)(a) CSA 2000 i.e. discharging functions of local authorities in connection with placing of children with foster parents.

Fostering Service Provider

- A fostering service provider means:
  - In relation to a fostering agency, the registered person
  - In relation to a local authority fostering service, a local authority

Looked After [s.22 CA 1989]

- A child who is 'looked after by a local authority may be 'accommodated', 'in care' or 'remanded / detained.
- Accommodation is a voluntary arrangement, the local authority does not gain parental responsibility and no notice is required for removal of the child.
- In care means that a court has made a child subject of a Care Order which gives the local authority parental responsibility and (some) authority to limit the parents' exercise of their continuing parental responsibility.
- The local authority has specific authority to detain those who fall into the third category (though with the exception of Emergency Protection Orders, the local authority does not gain parental responsibility) who may do so because of:
  - Remand by a court following criminal charges
  - Detention following arrest by police
  - An Emergency Protection Order or Child Assessment Order
  - A 'criminal' Supervision Order with a residence requirement

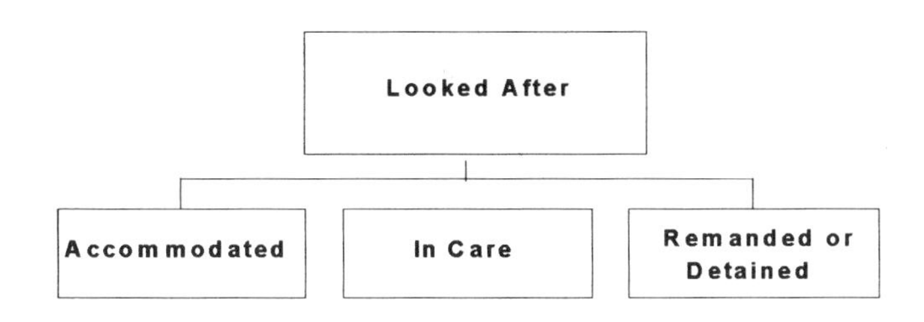

Parent [Reg. 2 Fostering Services Regulations 2002]

- A parent, in relation to a child, includes any person who has parental responsibility for her/him.

Registered Manager [Reg. 2 Fostering Services Regulations 2002]

- The registered manager means the person who is registered under Part II CSA 2000 as the manager of that agency.

Registered Person [Reg. 2 Fostering Services Regulations 2002]

- The registered person means any person who is the registered provider or the registered manager of the fostering agency.

Registered Provider [Reg. 2 Fostering Services Regulations 2002]

- The registered provider means the person who is registered under Part II of the CSA 2000 as the person carrying on the fostering agency.

NB. *In the case of a voluntary organisation which places children with foster parents under s.59(1) CA 1989, S.121(4) CSA 2000 defines the 'person carrying on a fostering agency' as the voluntary organisation itself.*

Routes Into Foster Care

Accommodating a Child [s.20 CA 1989]

- One of the family support services the local authority must provide is that of 'accommodating' (in family or residential settings) anyone under 18 'in need' who requires it as a result of:
  - There being no person with parental responsibility for her/him
  - S/he being lost or having been abandoned or
  - The person who has been caring for her/him being prevented temporarily or permanently (for whatever reason) from providing suitable care / accommodation
- This service is a completely voluntary arrangement and the local authority does not gain parental responsibility.
- A person with parental responsibility has the right to remove a child from such an arrangement [s.20(8) CA 1989] but:
  - A holder of a sole Residence Order could authorise the retention of a child in accommodation in spite of parent's wishes to remove [s.20(9) CA 1989]
  - A young person of 16 or 17 could overrule their parent's wishes to remove them [s.20(11) CA 1989]

- Anyone who does not have parental responsibility for a child but does have actual care of her/him may do what is reasonable in the circumstances to safeguard and promote the child's welfare [s.3 (5) CA 1989].
- If 'significant harm' seems likely, emergency protection measures could be used.

Accommodating a 16 or 17 Year Old [s.20 (3) CA 1989]

- A local authority must provide accommodation to a young person in the above age group if:
  - S/he is 'in need' and her/his welfare would otherwise be 'seriously prejudiced'.

Accommodating a Young Person Aged 16 – 20 Years Old [s.20 (5) CA 1989]

- A local authority may provide accommodation in any Community Home which accepts 16+ year olds if it considers it would safeguard or promote the young person's welfare.

Other Obligations To Accommodate [s.21 (1), (2) CA 1989]

- When asked, the local authority must 'accommodate' those:
  - Removed from home on an Emergency Protection Order, Child Assessment Order or an Interim Care Order

- In Police Protection
- Remanded by a court
- Detained under Police & Criminal Evidence Act 1984
- On a Supervision Order with residence requirements (Children & Young Persons Act 1969 [s.12AA]

Local Authority General Duties Towards Looked After Children [ss.22, 23, 24 & Sch.2 CA 1989]

- Safeguard and promote welfare and make reasonable efforts to allow child access to ordinary services as though still at home.
- Endeavour, unless not reasonably practical or consistent with welfare, to promote contact between child and:
  - Parents, and others with parental responsibility
  - Relatives, friends or persons connected with her/him
- Take reasonable steps to keep parents and those with parental responsibility informed of child's location.
- Before making any decision, ascertain wishes / feelings of:
  - Child
  - Parent/s and any others who have parental responsibility and relevant others
- Give due consideration to these views (having regard in case of child to level of understanding) religion, racial origin, cultural and linguistic background.

NB. A local authority may act contrary to above in order to protect public from serious injury.

- So far as is practical and consistent with welfare, place child with:
  - Parents
  - Someone who has parental responsibility
  - (For a child in care), any previous Residence Order holder
  - Relatives or friends or
  - Other person connected with her/him
- If a child has to be placed with strangers, ensure placement is near home and with any siblings.
- Prepare child for leaving looked after status.
- The local authority must also take reasonable steps to:
  - Reduce criminal / civil proceedings which might lead to Care or Supervision Orders
  - Avoid the use of secure accommodation
  - Encourage children not to commit crime

Additional Duties Towards a Child With a Disability

- Work with children who have a disability should be based on the principles that:
  - They are children first and their disability is a secondary, albeit significant issue
  - The aim should be to promote access to the same range of services for all

- Local authorities:
  - Must, so far as is practical, when they provide accommodation for a disabled child, ensure that the accommodation is not unsuitable for her/needs. [s.23(8) CA 1989]
  - Must maintain, for forward planning purposes, a register of children who have a disability [Sch. 2 para.2 CA 1989]
  - May assess a child's needs for the purpose of the Children Act at the same time as any assessment under certain other Acts, e.g. Education Act 1996. Sch.2 para. 3 CA 1989]
  - Must provide services for children who have a disability which are designed to minimise the effects of the disability and give them the opportunity to lead as normal lives as possible [Sch.2 para. 6 CA 1989]
- The rights of disabled children to consent to or refuse assessment / treatment or access their records is limited only by the general conditions regarding sufficient understanding which apply to other children under the Children Act 1989 [see companion personal guide to 'Child Protection' for further details].

Arranging Placements - Obligations of Responsible Authority

Arrangements for Placements of Children (General) Regulations 1991 as amended

- The above regulations describe the obligations of what is termed the 'responsible authority' when it makes a placement of a child.
- For a child looked after and placed by a local authority (in any placement including voluntary or private home) the local authority is the responsible authority.
- For a child accommodated and placed by a voluntary organisation (in whatever setting) the responsible authority is that voluntary organisation.

Placement Plan [Reg.3 Arrangement Regulations]

- Before a placement is made the responsible authority must, so far as is reasonably practical construct a written immediate and long term plan.
- Where impractical to do so before placement it must be done as soon as reasonably practical afterwards.
- The arrangements must normally be made with a person with parental responsibility or if there is no such person, with the current caregiver (for an individual of 16 or 17 accommodated despite parental objection, the arrangements should be with her/him).

Notification of Arrangements [Reg.5 Arrangement Regulations]

- So far as is reasonably practical, the responsible authority must provide advance written notification of the arrangements to place a child to:
  - Anyone whose wishes and feelings were sought prior to the placement by the local authority, voluntary organisation or private home provider respectively [ss.22(4), 61(2), 64(2) CA 1989]
  - The primary care trust (PCT) (or if there is no PCT, the health authority for the area in which the child is living) and if it is different for the area in which s/he is to be placed
  - Local education authority for the area in which the child is living and in which s/he is to be placed
  - The child's registered medical practitioner and, where applicable, any registered medical practitioner with whom the child is to be registered following the placement
  - Any person who was caring for the child immediately before the placement
  - Any person in whose favour there is a Contact Order (unless the child is 'in care')
  - Any person who has contact with the child as a result of a court order under s.34 CA 1989 (contact with a child in care by parents etc)

- The 'area authority' i.e. the local authority for the area in which the child is placed when this is not her/his own local authority

- Where impractical to provide advance notice it must be given as soon as possible after the placement begins.
- The responsible authority must also send with this notification:
  - As much of the placement plan as it believes will not prejudice the welfare of the child to those whose wishes / feelings were sought prior to placement
  - Such details as it believes they need to know to the other agencies / individuals cited above

Contents of Plan [Reg. 4 & Schs. 1, 2 & 3 Arrangement Regulations]

General Matters

- The aim of the placement and time scale should be contained in a written plan as should:
  - The proposed support for it
  - A contingency position if the desired plan fails
  - All identifiable needs including those arising from race, language, religion and culture
  - Agreed allocation of tasks
  - Dates of reviews

- Where the local authority is the responsible authority it must consider if it needs to seek a change in child's legal status e.g. application to discharge a Care Order.
- Arrangements for contact and any need to change them and the duty to promote contact (consistent with welfare) with family and relevant others must also be considered.
- Previous arrangements, any need for change and current immediate and long term proposals must be examined.
- In the case of a local authority, the possible need for an independent visitor considered.
- Whether arrangements are needed for child's departure from looked after or accommodated status.
- Whether plans are needed to find a permanent substitute family.

Health Matters

- Child's state of health and health history.

NB. *Records should include developmental history, illnesses, e.g. operations, immunisations, allergies, medication, appointments with G.P. etc. but not the antibody status of those known to be HIV positive which should be held on a 'need to know' basis only.*

- Effect of health / health history on her/his development.
- Current arrangements for medical / dental care and treatment, health and dental surveillance identifying any required changes.
- Any need for immunisations or sight or hearing screening.

Educational Matters

- Child's educational history and need to achieve continuity.
- Identification of educational needs and plan to meet them.
- Possible need to carry out assessment under the Education Act 1996 and meet any special educational needs thereby identified.

Matters to Be Included For Those Not In Care

- Address and type of accommodation to be provided and name of any person who will be responsible there, for the child on behalf of the responsible authority.
- Details of any services to be provided for child.
- Respective responsibilities of child, any parent of her/his, any non-parent who has parental responsibility detailing what delegation of day to day care those with parental responsibility have agreed with the responsible authority.
- Arrangements for involving above persons in decision making.
- Local authorities are obliged by s.20(6) & s.22(3)-(5) CA 1989 to involve children in decision making before accommodating them and to ascertain and give due consideration to the wishes and feelings of them and parents while looking after them.

- Voluntary organisations & private homes have comparable duties in respect of those for whom they are caring [s.61 (1) & (2), & s.64 (1) & (2) CA 1989 respectively].
- Arrangements for contact and any changes in these including (where appropriate) reasons why contact would not reasonably practical or would be inconsistent with the child's welfare, between child and:
  - Parents
  - Anyone else who has parental responsibility for them
  - Friends, relatives or persons connected with them
- Voluntary organisations & private homes must, unless it is not reasonably practical or consistent with welfare of child try to promote contact between her/him and the above persons.
- Where appropriate, confirmation that s.20 (11) CA 1989 (accommodation of a young person of 16 or over despite parental opposition) applies.
- The expected duration of the arrangements and steps which should be taken to end them, e.g. how to achieve rehabilitation with the person with whom child was living previously or with another suitable person.

Health Requirements [Reg. 7 Arrangements Regulations]

- Looked after children are especially vulnerable to a lack of continuity of health care.
- Unless completed within the 3 months prior to placement, a responsible authority must:
  - Ensure arrangements are made for assessment of child's health (may include a physical examination) by a doctor
  - Ask the doctor to provide a written assessment of the child health and any needs as listed in Sch. 2 Arrangement Regulations
- When it is not reasonably practical to make these arrangements before a placement they must be made as soon as practical after it begins.
- A child of sufficient understanding may refuse such an assessment [Reg.7 (4) Children Act (Miscellaneous Amendments) (England) Regulations 2002].

NB. *If the child's placement is likely to be short or in her/his own locality, it is usually preferable to use the child's own G.P. and s/he should be given the opportunity of using a doctor of the same sex.*

- A responsible authority must ensure that each child is provided during her/his placement with health care services including medical and dental care and treatment and advice and guidance on health, personal care and health promotion issues appropriate to her/his needs.

Establishment, Retention & Confidentiality of Records [Regs. 8 & 9 Arrangement Regulations]

- Each responsible authority must maintain written case records for every child it places.
- These records must include:
  - A copy of the 'placement plan' (see p.13)
  - Any report possessed about child's welfare
  - A copy of any records / documents connected with a case review
  - Details of contact arrangements, any contact or other court orders
  - Details of any arrangements for another person to act on behalf of the local authority or organisation which placed the child
- Records (originals, paper copies or other e.g. computer) must be kept by the responsible authority until the person is 75 or (should s/he die before 18 years of age) for 15 years after her/his death.
- Records must be stored securely and their contents treated as confidential unless:
  - A law allows access to them, e.g. A CAFCASS officer has a right of access to all records about a child belonging to or held by a local authority [s.42 CA 1989 as amended]
  - A court order obliges access to be given

Register of Placements [Reg. 10 Arrangements Regulations]

- A local authority is obliged to maintain a register of those placed in its area (by it and other responsible authorities) as well as those it places outside the area.
- A voluntary organisation and anyone carrying on a private home must also keep a register of those placed by them.
- Registers must contain considerable detail prescribed in paras. 3 & 4 of regulation 10 about the child and the placement.
- Details on the register must be retained until the child is 23 or if s/he dies before then, for 5 years after death.

Short -Term Placements [Reg.13 Arrangement Regulations as amended by Reg.3 The Children (Short-Term Placements) (Miscellaneous Amendments Regulations) 1995

- A series of placements in the same place may be treated as a single placement if:
  - All placements occur within a period of a year or less
  - No single placement lasts more than 4 weeks and
  - The total duration of the placements does not exceed 120 days

Limiting / Refusing Contact for Child In Care [s.34 CA 1989 & Contact with Children Regs. 1991]

Contact Plan [s.34 (2), (3) CA 1989]

- Courts must consider the proposed contact arrangements between child and parents and other involved relatives before making a Care Order. [s.34 (11) CA 1989.]
- Directions as to contact may be given on the court's initiative or as a response to an application made by :
  - The local authority
  - The child
  - Parents/guardian
  - A person who either held a Residence Order or had care of the child by virtue of an order made under the High Court's inherent jurisdiction, immediately before the Care Order was made
  - Any other person with court's permission

NB. *Contact may be by means of letters, telephone, photographs or any other method as well as visits.*

Local authorities are empowered to help with the cost of visiting residents where there would otherwise be undue hardship. [Sch.2 para.16 CA 1989].

Planned Refusal of Contact [s.34 (4) CA 1989]

- The court may, in response to an application by the local authority or child, make an order which allows the authority to refuse contact between the child and any of the persons listed in the contact plan section above.
- Orders under s.34 can be made at the same time the Care Order is made or later, and may be varied or discharged on the application of the local authority, child or the person named in the order.

Emergency Refusal of Contact [s.34 (6) CA 1989]

- A local authority can refuse to allow the normal 'reasonable contact', or that directed by the court if:
  - It is satisfied that it is necessary to do so to safeguard and promote the child's welfare and
  - Refusal is urgent and lasts no more than 7 days
- When a local authority has decided to refuse contact in this way, it must immediately notify in writing:
  - The child (if of sufficient understanding)
  - Her/his parents or guardian
  - Anyone who immediately before Care Order was made, held a Residence Order or had care by virtue of an order made under High Court's inherent jurisdiction and

- Anyone else whose wishes and feelings it considers relevant.

- Notification must contain as much of the following as the local authority believes these persons need to know:
  - The decision and the date it was made
  - Reasons for the decision, and, if applicable
  - How long it will last (max. 7 days)
  - How to challenge the decision

Departure from Terms of Court Order about Contact under s.34 [Reg. 3 Contact Regulations]

- A local authority can depart from the terms of a court order if the person named in the order agrees and:
  - Where the child is of sufficient understanding s/he also agrees
  - Written notification has been sent within 7 days

Other Variations or Suspension of Contact [Reg. 4 Contact Regulations]

- Where a local authority varies or suspends contact arrangements other than those made under s.34, to allow a person contact with a child in care, it must also provide written notification.

Independent Visitors [Sch. 2 Para.17 CA 1989 & Definition of Independent Visitors (Children) Regulations 1991]

- The local authority must appoint an independent visitor (whose role is to visit, advise and befriend) when a child is looked after by a local authority and:
  - Contact with a parent or other person who has parental responsibility has been infrequent or
  - S/he has not visited, been visited or lived with any of these people during the last 12 months and
  - It would be in the best interest of the child

NB. An independent visitor must be acceptable to a child and, if of sufficient understanding, s/he may refuse a proposed person. If the child has special needs, the visitor should have or be helped to develop relevant skills. An independent visitor is entitled to reclaim reasonable expenses from the local authority.

- A person may only be regarded as independent of the local authority if s/he is unconnected with the local authority i.e. is not a councillor, officer or their spouse.
- In the case of a child in accommodation other than that provided by the local authority, the visitor can only be regarded as independent if s/he is not a member, patron, trustee or employee (paid or not) of that organisation, nor a spouse of any of these persons.

NB. DH guidance suggests that 'spouse' could justifiably include a person in a stable cohabitation.

Reviews [s.26 CA 1989 & Review of Children's Cases Regulations 1991]

Review of Children's Cases Regulations 1991

- For a child looked after by a local authority, the responsible authority for ensuring compliance with the above regulations is that local authority.
- For a child not looked after by a local authority but provided with accommodation by a voluntary organisation, the responsible authority is that organisation.

Frequency of Reviews [Reg.2 Review Regulations 1991]

- Each case must be reviewed at the following intervals:
  - Within 4 weeks of a child becoming looked after or accommodated
  - Not more then 3 months after the first review
  - Not more than 6 months after the previous review

NB. These are minimum intervals and additional reviews may be convened in response to particular circumstances or at request of parent or child.

Health Reviews [Reg. 6 Review Regulations 1991 as amended]

- The responsible authority must make arrangements for those who continue to be looked after / accommodated by it to receive a health assessment (which may include a physical examination) and for a written report addressing matters listed in Sch.2 to be prepared at intervals of no more than:
  - 6 months for those under 5 years of age and
  - 12 months for those over 5
- The health assessment may be conducted by a registered medical practitioner to a registered nurse or midwife acting under her/his supervision and should inform the review of the plan for the future health of the child prepared under the Arrangement Regulations.
- A child of sufficient understanding may refuse to consent to such an assessment.

Procedures for Review, Consultation, Participation & Notification [Regs. 4, 7 & 10 Review Regulations 1991]

- Each responsible authority should have written procedures for the conduct of reviews which should be made known to service users.

- Before conducting any review the responsible authority must, unless it is not reasonably practical, seek and take into account the views of:
  - The child
  - Her/his parents
  - Any person other than a parent who has parental responsibility and
  - Anyone else whose views the local authority consider could be relevant to the review, e.g. foster parents, residential staff, teachers, health visitor, G.P.
- The above people must also, as far as is practical be:
  - Involved in the review, attending for as much of it as is thought appropriate
  - Notified of the results of the review and of any decisions taken as a result of it

NB. *A review's venue should be chosen, in consultation with parent/s, children and carers to encourage participation. Financial or practical support to attend should, where necessary, be provided. Any decision to exclude a parent or child from the review should be recorded and placed on file.*

- The responsible authority must ensure that information obtained as a result of a review, minutes of meetings and decisions made are recorded in writing.

Issues for Consideration Before or At Reviews [Regs.4, 5, 6 & Sch.1, 2 & 3 Review Regulations 1991]

- So far as is practical the responsible authority must consider:
  - Before reviews, making necessary preparations, e.g. initiating meetings of relevant staff of the responsible authority / other relevant persons and providing relevant information to potential participants
  - At reviews, the current arrangements, any relevant changes in child's circumstances and any consequent need to alter immediate or long term plan (including steps necessary to implement such change)
  - Names and addresses of people whose views should be taken into account
  - Explaining to child any steps s/he may take under the Act, e.g. where appropriate the right to apply with court's leave, for a s.8 order, and the existence of the complaints procedure
  - For those in care whether an application should be made to discharge the Care Order
  - Where the local authority is the responsible authority, whether it should seek a change in the child's legal status and/or appoint an independent visitor

- Contact arrangements and any need for change in relation to family and friends
- Educational needs, progress and development as well as any special arrangements which have been or need to be made, e.g. assessments under Education Act 1996
- Individual and as far as is practicable, family health history, current physical, emotional and mental health and their effects on development
- Existing arrangements for medical / dental treatment and surveillance, possible need for change including preventive measures such as vaccination / screening for vision or hearing and need for advice on health, personal care and health promotion issues
- Necessary arrangements for leaving care system
- Any need to plan for a permanent substitute family

NB. *The possibility of child needing to bring someone to support her/him should be considered as should any need to organise separate attendance by parents.*

Placement for Short Periods [Reg. 11 Review Regulations 1991 as amended by Reg.5 Children (Short-Term Placements) (Miscellaneous Amendments) Regulations 1995]

- A series of placements with the same caregiver or in the same home may be regarded as a single one for the purpose of these regulations if:
  - All the periods are contained within 12 months
  - No single period exceeds 4 weeks and
  - Total duration of the periods does not exceed 120 days

NB. In such short breaks / shared care arrangements, the time limit within which the first review must be held is 3 months from the beginning of the first of the short periods.

Looking After Children: Good Parenting, Good Outcomes [LAC System]

- Effective use of the LAC system, including proper completion of Planning and Review Forms and Assessment and Action Records ensures all the above obligations with respect to arrangements, placements and reviews are met.
- Foster parents should:
  - Encourage the child to share in the completion of the Records and in contributing to the Planning and Review Forms
  - If necessary, remind the social worker / case manager of the importance of use of the LAC system

NB. CAE publish a Personal Guide to the LAC System [see appendix 2].

General: [Regs. 1 – 4]

- The registered provider in relation to a fostering agency means a person who is registered under Part II of the CSA 2000 as the person carrying on the fostering agency [reg. 2].

Statement of Purpose & Children's Guide [Regs. 3 & 4]

- The fostering service provider must compile a 'statement of purpose' which includes:
    - The aims and objectives of the fostering service
    - A statement as to the facilities and services to be provided [reg.3(1)]
- The fostering service provider must provide a copy of the statement of purpose to the NCSC and make a copy of it available upon request for its inspection, by:
    - Any person working for the purpose of the fostering service
    - Any foster parent or prospective foster parent of the service
    - Any child placed with a foster parent by the fostering service and
    - The parent of any such child [reg.3(2)]

- The fostering service provider must also produce a 'children's guide' which includes:
  - A summary of the statement of purpose
  - A summary of the organisation's complaints procedure
  - Address and telephone number of the NCSC [reg.3(3)]
- The fostering service provider must provide copies of the children's guide to:
  - The NCSC
  - Each foster parent approved by the fostering service provider and
  - (Subject to age and understanding) each child placed by it [reg.3(4)]
- Subject to the appointment of a manager, the fostering service provider must ensure that the fostering service is at all times conducted in a manner which is consistent with its statement of purpose [reg.3 (5)].
- The fostering service provider must:
  - Keep under review and where appropriate, revise the statement of purpose and children's guide
  - Notify the NCSC within 28 days of any such revision and
  - Ensure that each foster parent approved by it and (subject to age and understanding), each child placed by it, receive the updated children's guide [reg. 4]

Registered Persons & Management of Local Authority Fostering Service: [Regs. 5– 10]

Fostering Agency: Fitness of Provider [Reg. 5 Fostering Services Regulations 2002]

- A person must not carry on a fostering agency unless s/he is fit to do so [reg.5 (1)].
- A person is not fit to carry on a fostering agency either as an individual, a partner or an organisation, unless all specified requirements are satisfied [reg.5(2)]
- The requirements are that:
  - The individual (all individuals in the case of a partnership or, in the case of an organisation, a nominated 'responsible individual' who supervises the management of the agency) is of integrity and good character
  - S/he is physically and mentally fit to carry on a fostering agency
  - Full and satisfactory information is available about the person as detailed in paras. 1 – 6 of Sch. 1 Fostering Services Regulations 2002 (prior to the implementation of ss.113 & 115 Police Act 1997) and paras. 1 and 3 – 7 (after their implementation) [reg.5(3)]

- The information required in respect of persons seeking to carry on, manage or work for the purposes for a fostering service is in Sch.1 as follows:
  - Positive proof of identity including a recent photograph
  - Either where the certificate is required for a purpose relating to s.115(5) of Police Act 1997 (registration under Part II of the 2000 Act), or the position falls within s.115(3) of that Act, an enhanced criminal record certificate issued under s.115 of that Act; or in any other case, a criminal record certificate issued under s.113 of that Act, including, where applicable, the matters specified in ss.113(3A) or 115(6A) of that Act
  - 2 written references, including a reference from the person's most recent employer, if any
  - Where a person has previously worked in a position whose duties involved work with children or vulnerable adults, so far as reasonably practicable verification of the reason why the employment or position ended
  - Documentary evidence of any relevant qualification
  - A full employment history, together with a satisfactory written explanation of any gaps in employment
  - Details of any criminal offences, of which the person has been convicted, including details of any convictions which are spent within the

meaning of s.1 Rehabilitation of Offenders Act 1974 (and which may be disclosed by virtue of the Rehabilitation of Offenders Act 1974 (Exceptions) Order 1975, or in respect of which s/he has been cautioned by a constable and which, at the time the caution was given, s/he admitted

- A person is not allowed to carry on a fostering agency if s/he is an un-discharged bankrupt or has made an arrangement with creditors in respect of which s/he has not been discharged [reg.5(2)].

Fostering Agency: Appointment of Manager [Reg. 6 Fostering Services Regulations 2002]

- The registered provider must appoint an individual to manage the fostering agency [reg.6 (1)].
- Where the registered provider is an organisation, it must not appoint the person who is the responsible individual as the manager, or where the registered provider is a partnership, it must not appoint any of the partners as the manager [reg.6(2)].
- Where the registered provider appoints a person to manage the fostering agency, s/he must immediately give notice to the NCSC of the:
  - Name of the person so appointed and
  - Date on which the appointment is to take effect [reg.6(3)]

Fostering Agency: Fitness of Manager [Reg. 7 Fostering Services Regulations 2002]

- A person must not manage a fostering agency unless s/he is fit to do so [reg.7 (1)].
- A person is not fit to manage a fostering agency unless:
  - S/he is of integrity and good character
  - Having regard to agency's size, statement of purpose and numbers and needs of children placed by it, s/he is physically and mentally fit for the role
  - Full and satisfactory information is available in relation to her/him as detailed in paras. 1 – 6 of Sch. 1 Fostering Services Regulations 2002 (prior to implementation of ss.113 & 115 Police Act 1997) and paras. 1 and 3 – 7 (after their implementation) [reg.7.(2)] (see page 36 for a summary of Sch.1 requirements)

Registered Person – General Requirements [Reg. 8 Fostering Services Regulations 2002]

- The registered provider and registered manager must, having regard to the agency's size, statement of purpose, and number and needs of children placed by it, and the need to safeguard and promote children placed, carry on

/ manage the fostering agency with sufficient care, competence and skill [reg.8(1)].

- From time to time, so as to ensure sufficient experience and skills necessary for carrying on the agency, appropriate training must be completed (as is relevant) by:
  - The registered provider (if s/he is an individual)
  - The responsible individual (and the responsibility for ensuring this rests with the organisation which engages her/him)
  - 1 member of any partnership [reg.8(2)]
- The registered manager must also undertake from time to time such training as is appropriate to ensure s/he has the experience and skills necessary for managing the fostering agency [reg.8(3)].

Notification of Offences [Reg. 9 Fostering Services Regulations 2002]

- Where the registered person or the responsible individual is convicted of any criminal offence in England or Wales or elsewhere, s/he must immediately give notice to the NCSC of the:
  - Date and place of the conviction
  - Offence of which s/he was convicted
  - Penalty imposed [reg.9(1)]

Local Authority Fostering Service: Manager [Reg. 10 Fostering Services Regulations 2002]

- Each local authority must appoint one of its officers to manage its fostering services and notify the NCSC of the name of the appointee and the date on which the appointment is to take effect [reg.10 (1)].
- The requirements in regulations 7, 8 and 9 (fitness of manger, general requirements of provider and manager, and notification of offences) are applicable to the manager of a local authority fostering service [reg.10 (2)].
- The local authority must immediately notify the NCSC if the fostering services manager ceases to manage that service.

Conduct of Fostering Service: [Regs. 11– 23]

Independent Fostering Agencies: Duty to Secure Welfare [Reg. 11 Fostering Services Regulations 2002]

- The registered person in respect of an independent fostering agency must ensure that:
  - The welfare of children placed or to be placed with foster parents is safeguarded and promoted at all times
  - Before making any decisions affecting a child placed or to be placed, due consideration is given to the child's wishes and feelings in the light of her/his age and understanding, religious persuasion, racial origin and cultural and linguistic background [reg.11(1)]

NB. A voluntary organisation which places children with foster parents under s.59 (1) CA 1989 has similar duties under s.61 CA 1989, as does a local authority under s.22 CA 1989.

Arrangements for the Protection of Children [Reg. 12 Fostering Services Regulations 2002]

- The fostering service provider must prepare and implement a written policy which:
  - Is intended to safeguard children placed with foster parents, from abuse or neglect and
  - Sets out the procedure to be followed in the event of any allegation of abuse or neglect [reg.12(1)]
- The above procedure must provide in particular for:
  - Liaison and co-operation with any local authority which is, or may be, making child protection enquiries (under any provision of the CA 1989) in relation to any child placed by the fostering service provider
  - Prompt referral to the area authority of any allegation of abuse or neglect affecting any child placed by the fostering service provider
  - Notification of instigation and outcome of any such enquiries involving a child placed by the fostering service provider, to the NCSC
  - Written records to be kept of any allegation of abuse or neglect, and of action taken in response
  - Consideration to be given to the measures which may be necessary to protect children placed with foster parents following an allegation of abuse or neglect

- Arrangements to be made for persons working for purpose of a fostering service, foster parents and children placed by the service, to have access to information which would enable them to contact the area authority and NCSC regarding any concern about child welfare or safety [reg.12(2)]

NB. The first and third of the above bullets and reference to the area authority in the final bullet do not apply to a local authority fostering service.

Behaviour Management & Absence from Foster Parent's Home [Reg.13 Fostering Services Regulations 2002]

- The fostering service provider must prepare and implement a written policy on acceptable measures of control, restraint and discipline of children placed with foster parents [reg.13 (1)].
- The fostering service provider must take all reasonable steps to ensure that:
  - No form of corporal punishment is used on any child placed with a foster parent
  - No child placed with foster parents is subject to any measure of control, restraint or disciple which is excessive or unreasonable and
  - Physical restraint is used on a child only when it is necessary to prevent likely injury to the child or other persons or likely serious damage to property [reg.13(2)]

- The fostering service provider must prepare and implement a written procedure to be followed if a child is absent from a foster parent's home without permission [reg.13 (3)].

Duty To Promote Contact [Reg. 14 Fostering Services Regulations 2002]

- The fostering service provider must (subject to the child's foster placement agreement and any court order about contact) promote contact between a child placed with her/him and the child's parents, relatives and friends unless such contact is not reasonably practicable or consistent with the child's welfare.

Health of Children Placed With Foster Parents [Reg. 15 Fostering Services Regulations 2002]

- The service provider must promote the health and development of children placed with carers and in particular ensure that each child is:
    - Registered with a GP and has access to such medical, dental, nursing, psychological and psychiatric advice, treatment and other services as s/he may require
    - Provided with such individual support, aids and equipment as s/he may require as result of any particular health needs or disability

- Provided with guidance, support and advice on health and personal care and health promotion issues appropriate to needs and wishes.

Education, Employment & Leisure Activities [Reg. 16 Fostering Services Regulations 2002]

- The service provider must promote the educational attainment of children who are placed with foster parents [reg.16 (1)].
- In particular, the service provider must:
    - Establish a procedure for monitoring the educational attainment, progress and school attendance of children placed with foster parents
    - Promote the regular school attendance and participation in school activities of school aged children placed with foster parents and
    - Provide foster parents with such information and assistance, including equipment, as may be necessary to meet the educational needs of children placed with them [reg.16(2)]
- The service provider must ensure any education it provides for any child placed with foster parents who is of compulsory school age but not attending, is efficient and suitable to the child's age, ability, aptitude, and any special educational needs s/he may have [reg.16(3)].

- The fostering service provider must ensure that foster parents promote the leisure interests of children placed with them [reg.16 (4)].
- Where any child placed with foster parents has attained the age where s/he is no longer required to receive full-time education, the fostering service provider must assist with making and implementing arrangements for the young person's education, training and employment [reg.16(5)].

Support, Training & Information for Foster Parents [Reg.17 Fostering Services Regulations 2002]

- The fostering service provider must provide foster parents with such training, advice, information and support (including support out of office hours) as appears necessary in the interests of children placed with them [reg.17(1)].
- The fostering service provider must take all reasonable steps to ensure that foster parents are familiar with and act in accordance with the policies established about child protection, behaviour management and absence without permission from a foster parent's home [reg.17(2)].
- The fostering service provider must ensure that in relation to any child placed or to be placed with her/him, a foster parent is given such information, which is kept up to date, as to enable her/him to provide appropriate care for the child.

- In particular each foster parent must be provided with appropriate information regarding the:
  - State of health and health needs of any child placed or to be placed with her/him
  - Arrangements for giving consent to child's medical / dental examination or treatment [reg.17(3)]

Independent Fostering Agencies: Complaints & Representations [Reg. 18 Fostering Services Regulations 2002]

- Representations, including complaints about discharge of a local authority's functions under Part III CA 1989, and the provision by a voluntary organisation of accommodation to any child not looked after by a local authority, are provided for by s.26 (3) – (8) and s.59 (4) CA 1989 respectively.
- For issues not covered by the Representation Procedure (Children) Regulations 1991, reg. 18 obliges the registered person of an independent fostering agency to establish a procedure for considering complaints made by or on behalf of children placed by the agency as well as foster parents approved by it [reg.18(1)].
- The procedure must in particular provide:
  - An opportunity for informal resolution of the complaint at an early stage
  - That no person subject of a complaint takes any part in its consideration other than if the

registered person considers it appropriate, at the informal resolution stage only

- For dealing with complaints about the registered person
- For complaints to be made by a person acting on behalf of a child
- For arrangements for the procedure to be made known to placed children, parents, and persons working for the purposes of the independent fostering agency [reg.18(2)]

- A copy of the procedure must be supplied on request to any of the above individuals and must include:
  - Name, address and phone number of NCSC and
  - Details of procedure (if any) notified to the registered person by the NCSC for making complaints to it about the agency [reg.18(3)]
- The registered person must ensure that a record is made of any complaint, the action taken in response and the outcome of the investigation [reg.18 (5)].
- The registered person must ensure that:
  - Children are enabled to make a complaint or representation and
  - No child is subject to any reprisal for making a complaint or representation [reg.18(6)]
- The registered person must supply the NCSC with an annual summary of complaints made in the preceding 12 months and the action taken in response [reg. 18(7)].

Staffing of Fostering Service [Reg. 19 Fostering Services Regulations]

- The fostering service provider must ensure that there is at all times a sufficient number of suitably qualified, competent and experienced persons working for the purposes of the fostering service having regard to the:
  - Size of the service, its statement of purpose and the number and needs of the children placed by it
  - Need to safeguard and promote the health and welfare of children placed with foster parents

Fitness of Workers [Reg. 20 Fostering Services Regulations]

- The fostering service provider must not, unless the person in question is fit to work for the purposes of the fostering service:
  - Employ a person to work for the purposes of the fostering service
  - Allow a person who is employed by someone other than the registered person to work in the service in a position in which s/he may in the course of her/his duties have regular contact with children placed by the service [reg.20(1)]
- A person is not 'fit' to work for the purposes of a fostering service unless:
  - S/he is of integrity and good character

- Has the qualifications, skills and experience necessary for the work s/he is to perform
- Is physically and mentally fit for the purposes of the work to be performed and
- Full and satisfactory information is available about her/him as per paras. 1 – 6 of Sch. 1 Fostering Services Regulations 2002 (prior to implementation of ss.113 & 115 Police Act 1997) and paras. 1 and 3 – 7 (following implementation) [reg.20(2) & (3)] (see page 36 for a summary of Sch.1 requirements)

- The service provider must also take reasonable steps to ensure non-employees who have less than regular contact with children placed are appropriately supervised.
- The service provider must not employ to work for the purposes of the fostering service as a manager or social worker (unless it is for 5 hours or less per week, on an occasional basis, or as a volunteer):
  - A foster parent approved by the fostering service
  - A member of the household of such a foster parent [reg.20(6)]

NB. This above does not apply to anyone already employed in one of the positions described on 01.04.02 [Reg.50 (7) Fostering Services Regulations 2002].

Employment of Staff [Reg. 21 Fostering Services Regulations 2002]

- The fostering service provider must:
    - Ensure all permanent appointments are subject to satisfactory completion of a probation period
    - Provide all employees with a job description [reg.21(1)]
- The fostering service provider must operate a disciplinary procedure which, in particular:
    - Provides for the suspension of an employee where necessary in the interests of the safety or welfare of children placed with foster parents
    - Provides that failure on the part of an employee to report to an appropriate person, an incident of abuse, or suspected abuse, of a child placed with foster parents is a ground on which disciplinary proceedings may be instituted [reg.21(2)]
- An appropriate person for the above purpose is:
    - In all cases, the registered person / manager of local authority fostering service, an officer of NCSC or area authority if applicable or a police officer or an officer of the NSPCC
    - For an employee of an independent fostering agency, an officer of the responsible authority and
    - For an employee of a fostering agency, an officer of the local authority in whose area the agency is situated [reg.21(3)]

- The fostering service provider must ensure that all persons employed by her/him:
    - Receive appropriate training, supervision and appraisal and
    - Are enabled from time to time to obtain further qualifications appropriate to the work they perform [reg.21(4)]

Records With Respect to Fostering Services [Reg. 22 & Sch. 2]

- The fostering service provider must maintain and keep up to date (as per Sch.2) a register which records, with respect to each child placed with a foster parent:
    - Date of her/his placement
    - Name and address of her/his foster parent
    - Date on which s/he ceased to be placed there
    - Address prior to the placement
    - Address on leaving the placement
    - Responsible authority (if it is not the fostering service provider)
    - The statutory provision under which s/he was placed with foster parents
- The fostering service provider must also maintain and keep up to date a record showing in respect of each person working for the fostering service provider:
    - Her/his full name

- Her/his sex
- Date of birth and
- Home address
- Qualifications relevant to and experience of work involving children
- Whether employed by the provider under a contract of service or a contract for services, or is employed by someone other than the fostering service provider
- Whether s/he works full or part-time and if part-time, the average number of hours worked per week

■ The fostering service provider must also maintain a record of all accidents occurring to children whilst placed with foster parents.

NB. All the above records must be retained for a period of 15 years from the date of last entry [reg.22 (2)].

Fitness of Premises [Reg. 23 Fostering Services Regulations 2002]

■ The fostering service provider must not use premises for the purposes of a fostering service unless the premises are suitable for the purpose of achieving the aims and objectives set out in the statement of purpose and must ensure that:

- There are adequate security arrangements at the premises, in particular that there are secure facilities for storage of records and
- Any records stored away from the premises are kept in conditions of appropriate security

Approval of Foster Parents [Regs. 24 - 32]

- The fostering service provider must establish at least 1 'fostering panel' [reg.24(1)]
- The service provider must appoint to chair it:
  - A senior member of staff of the service provider who is not responsible for day to day management of any person carrying out assessments of prospective foster parents or
  - Such other person, not being an employee, member, partner or director of the service provider, who has the skills and experience necessary for chairing the panel [reg.24(2)]
- The panel must consist of no more than 10 members including the chairperson and must include:
  - 2 social workers employed by the fostering service provider, 1 of whom has child care expertise and the other of whom has expertise in provision of a fostering service
  - In the case of a fostering agency, if the registered provider is an individual, that individual, if an organisation, at least 1 of its directors or the responsible individual and if a partnership, at least 1 of the partners
  - In the case of a local authority fostering service, at least 1 elected member

- At least 4 other persons (independent members) to include at least 1 person who is, or within the previous 2 years, has been a foster parent for a service provider other than the one whose panel is being established [reg.24(3)]

■ The service provider must appoint a member of the panel who will act as chairperson if the appointed individual is absent or the office is vacant [reg.24(4)].

■ A panel may be established jointly by any 2, and no more than 3 service providers, and if such a panel is established:

- The maximum number of members to be appointed is 11
- Each service provider must appoint 2 persons to the panel, 1 of whom has child care or fostering service experience, and the other of whom is (in the case of a fostering agency) one of those specified for single service providers or (in case of a local authority) an elected member
- By agreement between providers, there must be appointed a chairperson, at least 4 independent members including at least 1 who is, or has within previous 2 years, been a foster parent for a service provider other than any of those for whom panel is being established and a panel member to act as vice-chairperson [reg.24(5)]

■ A panel member must hold office for no more than 3 years and may not hold office for a panel of the same service provider for more than 2 consecutive terms [reg.24(6)].

- Any panel member may resign office at any time by giving a month's written notice to the fostering service provider [reg.24 (7)].
- Where a fostering service provider is of the opinion that any panel member is unsuitable or unable to remain in office, it may terminate her/his office at any time by giving written notice [reg.24 (8)].
- A person may not be appointed as an independent panel member if:
  - S/he is a foster parent approved by the fostering service provider
  - S/he is employed by the provider
  - S/he is concerned in the management of the fostering service provider
  - In the case of a local authority fostering service, s/he is an elected member of the local authority or
  - In the case of a fostering agency, s/he is related to an employee of the registered provider, or to any person concerned in the management of the fostering agency [reg.24(9)]
- For the above purposes, a 'person A' is related to a 'person B' if s/he is a member of the household of, or married to B, the son, daughter, mother, father, sister or brother or B or the son ,daughter, mother, father, sister or brother of the person to whom B is married [reg.24(10)]

Meetings of Fostering Panel [Reg. 25 Fostering Services Regulations 2002]

- No business may be conducted by a panel unless at least 5 of its members, including the appointed chairperson (or vice-chairperson), at least 1 of the social workers employed by the fostering service and at least 2 of the independent members, meet as a panel [reg.25 (1)].
- In the case of a joint panel, no business may be conducted unless at least 6 members, including appointed chair or vice-chairperson and 1 social worker from each fostering service meet as a panel [reg.25(3).
- A panel must make a written record of its proceedings and the reasons for its recommendation [reg.25 (2)].

Functions of Fostering Panel [Reg. 26 Fostering Services Regulations 2002]

- The functions of the fostering panel are:
  - To consider each application for approval and to recommend (to the service provider) whether or not a person is suitable to act as a foster parent
  - Where it recommends approval, to recommend the terms on which the approval is to be given
  - To recommend whether a person remains suitable to act as a foster parent, and whether the terms of her/his approval remain appropriate, on the first routine review and on any other occasion when it is invited to do so (see below)

- To consider further, any written representations challenging a decision by the service provider not to approve an individual, (see below) which are referred to it by the service provider
- To consider further, any written representations challenging a decision by the service provider to terminate, or revise the terms of, the approval of an individual, (see below) which are referred to it by the service provider [reg.26(1)]

■ The fostering panel must also:

- Advise on the procedures under which 'regulation 29' reviews (see below) are carried out by the fostering service provider and periodically monitor their effectiveness
- Oversee the conduct of assessments carried out by the fostering provider and
- Give advice and make recommendations on such matters or cases as the fostering service provider may refer to it [reg.26(2)]

Assessment of Prospective Foster Parents [Reg. 27 Fostering Services Regulations 2002]

■ The fostering service provider must carry out an assessment of any person whom it considers may be suitable to become a foster parent, in accordance with regulation 27 [reg.27 (1)].

- If the fostering service provider considers that a person may be suitable to act as a foster parent, it must:
  - Obtain the information specified in Sch.3 relating to the prospective foster parent and other members of her/his household and family and any other information it considers relevant
  - Interview at least 2 persons nominated by the prospective foster parent to provide personal references for her/him, and prepare written reports of the interviews
  - (Unless the service provider is a local authority and applicant lives within that authority), consult with and take into account the views of, the local authority where the prospective foster parents live
  - Having regard to these matters, consider whether the prospective foster parents is suitable to act as a foster parent and whether her/his household is suitable for any child in respect of whom approval may be given
  - Prepare a report on her/him which includes the matters specified in para. 4 (summarised below)
  - Refer the report to the fostering panel and notify the prospective foster parent accordingly [reg.27(2)]
- Sch.3 specifies the following information which is required with respect to prospective foster parent:
  - Full name, address and date of birth

- Details of health (supported by a medical report), personality, marital status and details of current and any previous marriage or similar relationship
- Particulars of other adults in her/his household
- Particulars of the children in her/his family, whether or not members of the household and any other children in the household
- Particulars of her/his accommodation
- Her/his religious persuasion and capacity to care for a child from any particular religious persuasion
- Racial origin, cultural and linguistic background and capacity to care for a child from any particular such background
- Past and present employment or occupation, standard of living and leisure activities and interests
- Previous experience (if any) of caring for her/his own and other children
- Skills, competence and potential relevant to her/his capacity to care effectively for a child placed with her/him
- The outcome of any request or application made by her/him or any other household member to foster or adopt, register for child minding or day care, including particulars of any previous approval or refusal of approval relating to her/him or to any other household members

- Names and addresses of 2 persons who will provide personal references for the prospective foster parent

■ Sch.3 also requires, in relation to the prospective foster parent, either an enhanced criminal records certificate issued under s.115 PA 1997 (to include matters specified under s.115(6A) of that Act) or where the above certificate is not available because any provision of the PA 1997 has not been brought into force, then:

- In relation to each household member aged 18 or over details of any criminal offences of which the person has been convicted , including 'spent' convictions which may be disclosed by virtue of the Rehabilitation of Offenders Act 1974 (Exceptions) Order as amended

■ The report for panel referred to above must include the following matters in relation to the prospective foster parent:

- The information required by Sch.3 and any other information the fostering service provider considers relevant
- The fostering service provider's assessment of her/his suitability to act as a foster parent and
- The fostering service provider's proposals about the terms and conditions of any approval [reg.27(4)]

- A person must not be regarded as suitable to act a foster parent if s/he or any member of the household aged 18 or over:
  - Has been convicted of a specified offence committed at the age of 18 or over or
  - Has been cautioned by police in respect of any such offence, which at the time the caution was given, s/he admitted [reg.27(5)]
- The fostering service provider may though consider such a person as suitable to act / continue to act as a foster parent for a particular named child if the service provider is satisfied that the welfare of that child or those children requires it and the person or a member of her/his household is a relative of the child or the person is already acting as a foster parent for the child [reg.27 (6)].

NB. For the purposes of regulation 27, 'specified offence' is defined in regulation 27(7) Fostering Services Regulations 2002.

Approval of Foster Parents [Reg. 28 Fostering Services Regulations 2002]

- A fostering service provider must not approve a person who has been approved as a foster parent by another fostering service provider and whose approval has not been terminated [reg.28 (1)].
- A fostering service provider must not approve a person as a foster parent unless:

- It has completed its assessment of her/his suitability and
- Its fostering panel has considered the application [reg.28(2)]

■ A fostering service provider must, in deciding whether to approve a person as a foster parent and as to terms of approval, take into account the recommendation of its fostering panel [reg.28(3)].

■ No member of its fostering panel may take part in any such decision made by a fostering service provider.

■ If a fostering service provider decides to approve a person as a foster parent, it must:

- Give her/him written notice specifying terms of approval e.g. in respect of a named child/ren, number and age range of children, or of placements of any particular kind, or in any particular circumstances
- Enter into a written agreement covering the matters specified in Sch.5 below (the foster care agreement) [reg.28(5)]

■ Sch.5 specifies the matters and obligations in foster care agreements as follows:

- Terms of foster parent's approval
- Amount of support and training to be given to foster parent
- Procedure for review of approval

- Procedures in connection with placement of children and matters to be included in any foster placement agreement
- Arrangements for meeting any legal liabilities of the foster parent arising by reason of a placement
- Procedure available to foster parents for making representations
- To give written notice to the service provider, with full particulars of any intended change of address or household composition, any other change in personal circumstance and any other event affecting capacity to care for any child placed or suitability of household and any request or application to adopt or for registration for child minding or day care
- Not to administer corporal punishment to any child placed with her/him
- To ensure any information relating to a placed child, to the child's family or any other person, given in confidence in connection with the placement, is kept confidential and not disclosed to anyone without consent of the service provider
- To comply with the terms of any foster placement agreement
- To care for any child as if s/he were a member of the family and to promote her/his welfare having regard to the long and short-term plans for her/him

- To comply with policies and procedures of the fostering service provider issued under regulations 12 and 13 (see above)
- To co-operate as reasonably required with the NCSC and in particular, to allow a person authorised by the NCSC to interview her/him and visit her/his home at any reasonable time
- To keep the fostering service provider informed about child's progress and notify it immediately of any significant events affecting the child
- To allow any child placed with her/him to be removed from her/his home if regulation 36 applies (i.e. the placement is no longer considered suitable – see below)

■ If a fostering service provider considers that a person is not suitable to act as a foster parent it must:

- Give him written notice that it proposes not to approve her/him, together with its reasons and a copy of the fostering panel's recommendations
- Invite her/him to submit written representations within 28 days of date of the notice [reg.28 (6)]

■ If the fostering service provider does not receive any representations within 28 days, it may proceed to make its decision [reg.28 (7)].

■ If the fostering service provider receives any written representations within 28 days, it must:

- Refer the case to the fostering panel for further consideration and

- Make its decision, taking into account any fresh recommendations made by the fostering panel [reg.28(8)]

■ As soon as practicable after making the decision with respect to approval, the fostering service provider must notify the prospective foster parent in writing and:

- If the decision is to approve the person, provide terms of approval as described above
- If the decision is not to approve the person, provide written reasons for its decision [reg.28(9)]

Reviews & Terminations of Approval [Reg. 29 Fostering Services Regulations 2002]

■ The service provider must review approval of each foster parent in accordance with regulation 29 [reg.29 (1)].

■ A review must take place not more that a year after approval, and thereafter whenever the service provider considers it necessary, but at intervals of not more than a year [reg.29 (2)].

■ When undertaking a review, the fostering service provider must:

- Make such enquiries and obtain such information as it considers necessary to review whether the person continues to be suitable to act as a foster parent and his household continues to be suitable

- Seek and take into account views of foster parent, and (subject to age and understanding) any child placed with the foster parent and any responsible authority which has within the preceding year placed a child with the foster parent [reg.29(3)]

- At the conclusion of the review the service provider must prepare a written report, setting out whether:
  - The person continues to be suitable to be a foster parent and her/his household continues to be suitable
  - The terms of her/his approval continue to be appropriate [reg.29(4)]

- The fostering service provider must, for the first review and may, on any subsequent review, refer its report to the fostering panel for consideration [reg.29 (5)].

- If the fostering service provider decides, taking into account any recommendation made by fostering panel, that the foster parent and household continue to be suitable and terms of approval continue to be appropriate, it must give written notice to the foster parent of its decision [reg.29(6)].

- If, taking into account any recommendation made by the panel, the service provider is no longer satisfied the foster parent and her/his household continue to be suitable, or that terms of approval are appropriate, it must:
  - Notify the foster parent in writing that it proposes to terminate, or revise terms of her/his approval as the case may be, together with its reasons, and

- Invite her/him to submit any written representations within 28 days of the date of the notice [reg.29(7)]

- If the service provider does not receive any representations within 28 days it may proceed to make its decision [reg.29 (8)].

- If the service provider does receive any written representations within 28 days, it must:
  - Refer the case to the fostering panel for its consideration; and
  - Make its decision, taking into account any recommendation made by the panel [reg.29(9)]

- As soon as practicable after making its final decision (with or without panel input as described above) the service provider must write to the foster parent stating:
  - The foster parent and her/his household continue to be suitable, and the terms of the approval continue to be appropriate or
  - Her/his approval is terminated from a specified date, and the reasons for the termination or
  - The revised terms of the approval and the reasons for the revision [reg.29(10)]

- A foster parent may give notice in writing to the fostering service provider at any time that s/he no longer wishes to act as a foster parent, whereupon her/his approval is terminated with effect from 28 days from the date on which the notice is received by the fostering service provider [reg.29(11)].

- A copy of any notice given under this regulation shall be sent to the responsible authority for any child placed with the foster parent (unless the responsible authority is also the fostering service provider), and the area authority [reg.29 (12)].

Case Records Relating to Foster Parents & Others [Reg. 30 Fostering Services Regulations 2002]

- A fostering service provider must maintain a case record for each foster parent approved by it which must include the following documents:
    - Notice of approval given under regulation 28(5)(a)
    - Foster care agreement
    - Any report of a review of approval prepared under regulation 29(4)
    - Any notice given under regulation 29(10)
    - Any agreement entered into in accordance with regulation 38(1)(a)
    - The report prepared under regulation 27(2)(e) and any other reports submitted to the fostering panel and
    - Any recommendations made by the fostering panel

- The case record must also include the following information:
  - A record of each placement with the foster parent, including name, age and sex of each child placed, dates on which each placement began and terminated and the circumstances of the termination
  - The information obtained by the fostering service provider in relation to the assessment and approval of the foster parent and in relation to any review or termination of the approval
- A local authority is obliged to maintain a case record for each person with whom a child is placed under regulation 38(2) (i.e. 'immediate' placements) to include:
  - The agreement entered into in accordance with regulation 38(2)(b)
  - A record in relation to the placement, including the name, age and sex of each child placed, dates on which the placement began and terminated, and the circumstances of the termination and
  - The information obtained in relation to the enquiries carried out under regulation 38(2)
- The fostering service provider shall compile a record for each person whom it does not approve as a foster parent, or who withdraws her/his application prior to approval, which must include in relation to her/him:
  - The information obtained in connection with the assessment

- Any report submitted to the fostering panel and any recommendation made by the fostering panel and
- Any notification given under regulation 28

Register of Foster Parents [Reg. 31 Fostering Services Regulations 2002]

- The fostering service provider must enter in a register kept for the purpose the:
  - Name, address, date of birth and sex of each foster parent
  - Date of her/his approval and of each review of her/his approval and
  - Current terms of her/his approval
- In addition, a local authority must enter in its register, the:
  - Name and address of each person with whom it has placed a child under regulation 38(2)
  - Date of each agreement entered into in accordance with regulation 38(2)(b) and
  - Terms of any such agreement for the time being in force

Retention & Confidentiality of Records [Reg. 32 Fostering Services Regulations 2002]

- Records compiled in relation to a foster parent under regulation 30(1), and any entry relating to her/him in the register maintained under regulation 31(1) must be retained for at least 10 years from the date on which approval is terminated [reg. 32(1)]
- Records compiled by a local authority under regulation 30(4) in relation to a person with whom a child is placed under regulation 38(2), and any entry relating to such a person in the register maintained under regulation 31(1), must be retained for at least 10 years from the date on which the placement is terminated [reg.32(2)].
- Records compiled under regulation 30(5) must be retained for at least 3 years from refusal or withdrawal, of the application to become a foster parent [reg.32(3)].
- These requirements may be complied with by retaining the original written records or copies, or by keeping all or part of the information contained in them in another accessible form e.g. computer record [reg. 32(4)].
- Any records or register maintained in accordance with regulation 30 or 31must be kept securely and may not be disclosed to any person except in accordance with any:
    - Provision of, or made under, or by virtue of, a statute under which access to such records is authorised or any
    - Court order authorising access to such records

Placements [Regs. 33 – 40]

General Duty of Responsible Authority [Reg. 33]

- A responsible authority must not place a child with a foster parent unless it is satisfied that:
  - It is the most suitable way of performing its duty under (as the case may be) section 22(3) or 61(1)(a) and (b) of CA 1989 and
  - A placement with the particular foster parent is the most suitable placement having regard to all the circumstances

Making of Placements [Reg. 34]

- Except in the case of an emergency or immediate placement under regulation 38, a responsible authority may only place a child with a foster parent if:
  - The foster parent is approved by the responsible authority proposing to make the placement or provided the conditions specified in reg.34(2) (immediately below) are satisfied, by another fostering service provider
  - The terms of his approval are consistent with the proposed placement and s/he has entered into a foster care agreement [reg.34(1)]

- The conditions referred to in reg.34(1)) are:
    - That the service provider by whom the foster parent is approved, consents to the placement
    - That any other responsible authority which already has a child placed with the foster parent, consents to the placement
    - Where applicable, the area authority is consulted, its views taken into account, and it is given notice if the placement is made and
    - (Where the foster parent is approved by an independent fostering agency), requirements of regulation 40 are complied with
- Before making a placement, the responsible authority must enter into a written foster placement agreement with the foster parent relating to the child, which covers the matters specified in Schedule 6 [reg.34(3)].
- Schedule 6 specifies the following 8 matters and obligations to be covered in foster placement agreements.
- There must be a statement by the responsible authority containing all information the authority considers necessary to enable the foster parent to care for the child, in particular information as to:
    - The authority's arrangements for the child and the objectives of the placement in the context of its plan for the care of the child

- Child's personal history, religious persuasion, cultural and linguistic background and racial origin
- Child's state of health and identified health needs
- Safety needs of the child, including any need for any special equipment or adaptation
- Child's educational needs and
- Any needs arising from any disability of child

- The responsible authority's arrangements for the financial support of the child during the placement.
- The arrangements for giving consent to the medical or dental examination or treatment of the child.
- The circumstances in which it is necessary to obtain in advance the approval of the responsible authority for the child to take part in school trips, or to stay overnight away from the foster parent's home.
- The arrangements for visits to the child by the person authorised by or on behalf of the responsible authority, and the frequency of visits and reviews under the Review of Children's Cases Regulations 1991 as amended.
- The arrangements for the child to have contact with his parents and any other specified persons, and details of any court order relating to contact.
- Compliance by the foster parent with the terms of the foster care agreement
- Co-operation by the foster parent with the responsible authority regarding any arrangements it makes for the child.

Supervision of Placements [Reg. 35]

- A responsible authority must satisfy itself that the welfare of each child placed by it continues to be suitably provided for by the placement, and for that purpose the authority must make arrangements for a person authorised by the authority to visit the child, in the home in which he is placed:
  - From time to time as circumstances may require
  - When reasonably requested by the child or the foster parent and
  - In any event (subject to regulation 37) in the first year of the placement, within 1 week from its beginning and then at intervals of not more than 6 weeks and subsequently, at intervals of not more than 3 months [reg.35(1)]
- In the case of an immediate placement under regulation 38, the local authority must arrange for the child to be visited at least once in each week during the placement [reg.35 (2)].
- On each occasion on which the child is visited under this regulation the responsible authority must ensure that the person it has authorised to carry out the visit:
  - Sees the child alone unless s/he, being of sufficient age and understanding to do so, refuses and
  - Prepares a written report of the visit

Termination of Placements [Reg. 36 Fostering Services Regulations 2002]

- A responsible authority must not allow the placement of a child with a particular person to continue if it appears to them that the placement is no longer the most suitable way of performing its duty under (as the case may be) section 22(3) or 61(1)(a) and (b) of the CA 1989 [reg.36(1)].
- Where it appears to an area authority that the continuation of a placement would be detrimental to the welfare of the child concerned, the area authority must remove the child forthwith [reg. 36(2)].
- An area authority which removes a child under reg.36 (2) must forthwith notify the responsible authority [reg.36 (3)].

Short-Term Placements [Reg. 37 Fostering Services Regulations 2002]

- This regulation applies where a responsible authority has arranged to place a child in a series of short-term placements with the same foster parent and the arrangement is such that:
    - No single placement is to last for more than 4 weeks and
    - The total duration of the placements is not to exceed 120 days in any period of 12 months [reg.37(1)]

- A series of short-term placements to which this regulation applies may be treated as a single placement for the purposes of these regulations, but with the modifications set out in paragraphs (3) and (4) immediately below [reg.37(2)].

NB. With respect to a series of short-term placements, reg. 35(1)(c)(i) and (ii) are modified to apply as if they required arrangements to be made for visits to the child on a day when s/he is in fact placed ('a placement day') within the first 7 placement days of a series of short-term placement and thereafter, if the series of placements continues, at intervals of not more than 6 months or, if the interval between placements exceeds six months, during the next placement [reg.37(3)].

- Regulation 41 will apply as if it required arrangements to be made for visits to the child on a placement day within the first 7 placement days of a series of short-term placements [reg.37(4)].

Emergency & Immediate Placements by Local Authorities [Reg. 38 Fostering Services Regulations 2002]

- Where a child is to be placed in an emergency, a local authority may, for a period not exceeding 24 hours, place the child with any foster parent approved by the local authority or any other fostering service provider provided that:

- The foster parent has made a written agreement with the local authority to carry out the duties specified below and
- The local authority is satisfied as to the provisions of regulation 33(a) (i.e. this is the most suitable way of performing its duty) [reg.38(1)]

■ Where a local authority is satisfied that the immediate placement of a child is necessary, it may place the child with a person who is not a foster parent after interviewing her/him, inspecting the accommodation and obtaining information about other persons living in her/his household, for a period not exceeding 6 weeks, provided that:

- The person is a relative or friend of the child
- The person has made a written agreement with the local authority to carry out the duties specified below and the local authority is satisfied as to the provisions of regulation 33(a) (i.e. it is the most suitable way of performing its duty)

■ The duties referred to in reg.38 (1)(a) and (2)(b) are:

- To care for the child as if s/he were a member of that person's family
- To permit any person authorised by the local authority or (if applicable) the area authority, to visit the child at any time
- Where reg. 36 applies, to allow the child to be removed at any time by the local authority or (if applicable) the area authority

- To ensure any information that person may acquire relating to child, family or any other person given to him in confidence in connection with the placement is kept confidential and not disclosed, except to, or with the agreement of, the local authority; to allow contact with child in accordance with terms of any court order relating to contact or any arrangements made or agreed by local authority [reg.38(3)]

- Where a local authority makes a placement under this regulation outside their area it must notify the area authority [reg.38 (4)].

Placements Outside England [Reg. 39 Fostering Services Regulations 2002]

- A voluntary organisation must not place a child outside British Islands (UK, Channel Islands and Isle of Man) [reg.40 (1)].
- Where a responsible authority makes arrangements to place a child outside England it must ensure, so far as reasonably practicable, that requirements which would have applied under these regulations had the child been placed in England, are complied with [reg.39(2)].
- In the case of a placement by a local authority outside England or Wales, reg.39 (3) is subject to provisions of paragraph 19 of Schedule 2 CA 1989 (arrangements to assist children to live abroad) which require court approval in the case of a child in care and approval of all those who hold parental responsibility in all other cases.

Independent Fostering Agencies – Discharge of Local Authority Functions [Reg. 40 Fostering Services Regulations 2002]

- A local authority may make arrangements in accordance with this regulation for the duties imposed on it as a responsible authority by regulations 34, 35, 36(1) and 37and (where reg.40(3) below applies, 33(b)) to be discharged on its behalf by a registered person [reg.40(1)].
- Subject to reg.40(3), no arrangements may be made under this regulation in respect of a particular child, unless a local authority has performed its duties under regulation 33 in relation to that child [reg.40(2)].
- Where a local authority makes arrangements with a registered person for the registered person to provide foster parents for the purposes of a short-term placement within the meaning of reg.37 (1), the local authority may also make arrangements for the registered person to perform the local authority's duty under regulation 33(b) in relation to that placement on its behalf [reg.40 (3)].
- No arrangements may be made under this regulation unless a local authority has entered into a written agreement with the registered person which sets out:
  - Which of its duties the local authority proposes to delegate in accordance with this regulation
  - The services to be provided to the local authority by the registered person

- The arrangements for the selection by the local authority of particular foster parents from those approved by the registered person
- A requirement for the registered person to submit reports to the local authority on any placement as may be required by the authority, and in particular following any visit carried out under reg.35 and
- The arrangements for the termination of the agreement [reg.40(4)]

■ Where a local authority proposes to make an arrangement under this regulation in respect of a particular child the local authority shall enter into an agreement with the registered person in respect of that child which sets out:

- Details of the particular foster parent with whom the child is to be placed
- Details of any services the child is to receive
- The terms (including as to payment) of the proposed foster placement agreement
- The arrangements for record keeping about the child, and for the return of records at the end of the placement
- A requirement for the registered person to notify the local authority immediately in the event of any concerns about the placement and
- Whether and on what basis other children may be placed with the foster parent [reg.40(5)]

- A foster parent with whom a child is placed in accordance with arrangements made under this regulation is, in relation to that placement, to be treated for purposes of paragraph 12(d) of Schedule 2 CA 1989 as a local authority foster parent [reg.40(6)].
- A local authority shall report to the NCSC any concerns it may have about the services provided by a registered person [reg.40 (7)].

In this regulation 'registered person' means a person who is the registered person in respect of an independent fostering agency [reg.40 (8)].

Local Authority Visits [Reg 41]

Local Authority Visits to Children Placed by Voluntary Organisations [Reg. 41 Fostering Services Regulations 2002]

- Every local authority must arrange for a person authorised by the local authority to visit every child who is placed with a foster parent within its area by a voluntary organisation as follows:
  - Subject to reg. 37(4) (special short-term placement arrangement), within 28 days of the placement
  - Within 14 days of receipt of a request from the voluntary organisation which made the placement to visit a child
  - As soon as reasonably practicable if it is informed that the welfare of the child may not be being safeguarded or promoted, and
  - At intervals of not more than 6 months where the local authority is satisfied, following a visit to a child under this regulation that the child's welfare is being safeguarded and promoted [reg.41(1)]
- Every local authority must ensure that a person carrying out a visit in accordance with reg.41(1):
  - Sees the child during the course of the visit, or if the child is not there, makes arrangements to see the child as soon as reasonably practicable, and

- Takes steps to discover whether the voluntary organisation which placed the child have made suitable arrangements to perform their duties under these regulations, and those under s.61CA 1989 [reg.41(2)]

- A local authority must report to the NCSC any concerns it may have about the voluntary organisation [reg.41 (3)].

Fostering Agencies - Miscellaneous [Regs. 42 – 49]

Review of Quality of Care [Reg. 42]

- The registered person must establish and maintain a system for:
  - Monitoring the matters set out in Schedule 7 at appropriate intervals and
  - Improving the quality of foster care provided by the fostering agency [reg.42(1)]
- The matters in Sch.7 to be monitored by the registered person are:
  - Compliance in relation to each child placed with foster parents, with the foster placement agreement and the responsible authority's plan for the care of the child
  - All accidents, injuries and illnesses of children placed with foster parents
  - Complaints in relation to children placed with foster parents and their outcomes
  - Any allegations or suspicions of abuse in respect of children placed with foster parents and the outcome of any investigation
  - Recruitment records and conduct of required checks of new workers
  - Notification of events listed in Sch.8

- Any unauthorised absence from the foster home of a child accommodated there
- Use of any measure of control, restraint or discipline in respect of children accommodated in a foster home
- Medication, medical treatment and first aid administered to any child placed with foster parents
- Where applicable, the standard of any education provided by the fostering service
- Records of assessments
- Records of fostering panel meetings
- Duty rosters of persons working for the fostering agency, as arranged and as actually worked
- Records of appraisal of employees
- Minutes of staff meetings

■ The registered person must supply to the NCSC a report in respect of any review conducted by her/him for the purposes of reg. 42(1) and make a copy of the report available upon request to the persons mentioned in reg.3 (2) (persons working for purpose of service, actual or prospective foster parent, foster child and her/his parent) [reg.42 (2)].

■ The system referred to in reg.42 (1) must provide for consultation with foster parents, children placed with foster parents, and their responsible authority (unless, in the case of a fostering agency which is a voluntary organisation, it is also the responsible authority).

Notifiable Events [Reg. 43]

- If, in relation to a fostering agency, any of the events listed in column 1 of the table in Sch.8 (summarised on the next two pages) takes place, the registered person must without delay notify the persons indicated in respect of the event in column 2 of the table [reg.43(1)].
- Any notification made in accordance with this regulation which is given orally must be confirmed in writing [reg.43].

Events	To be notified to					
	NCSC	Responsible authority	Secretary of State	Area authority	Police	Health authority
Child's death	✓	✓	✓	✓		✓
Referral to Sec of State re: individual	✓	✓				
Serious illness / accident of placed child	✓	✓				
Serious infectious disease	✓	✓				✓
Allegation of serious crime by child		✓			✓	
Involvement or suspected involvement of child in prostitution	✓	✓		✓	✓	

Events	**To be notified to**					
	NCSC	**Responsible authority**	**Secretary of State**	**Area authority**	**Police**	**Health authority**
Serious incident involving police	✓	✓				
Absconding	✓	✓				
Any serious complaint re: foster parent	✓	✓				
Investigation & outcome any protection enquiry	✓	✓				

Financial Position [Reg. 44]

- The registered provider must carry on the agency in such manner as is likely to ensure it will be financially viable for the purpose of achieving the aims and objectives set out in its statement of purpose [reg.44(1)].
- The registered provider must:
  - Ensure that adequate accounts are maintained and kept up to date in respect of the fostering agency
  - Supply a copy of the accounts, certified by an accountant to the NCSC [reg.44(2)]
- The registered provider must, if the NCSC so requests, provide it with such information as it may require for the purpose of considering the financial viability of the fostering agency, including:
  - The annual accounts of the fostering agency, certified by an accountant
  - A reference from a bank expressing an opinion as to the registered provider's financial standing
  - Information as to the financing and financial resources of the fostering agency
  - Where the registered provider is a company, information as to any of its associated companies,
  - A certificate of insurance for the registered provider in respect of liability which may be incurred by her/him in relation to the fostering agency in respect of death, injury, public liability, damage or other loss [reg.44(3)]

NB. In this regulation, one company is associated with another if one of them has control of the other, or both are under the control of the same person [reg.44 (4)].

Notice of Absence [Reg. 45]

- Where the registered manager proposes to be absent from the agency for a continuous period of 28 days or more, the registered person must give notice in writing to the NCSC of the proposed absence [reg.45(1)].
- Except in an emergency, the notice referred to above must be given no later than 1 month before the proposed absence is to start, or within such shorter period as may be agreed with the NCSC, and the notice must specify:
    - Length or expected length of proposed absence
    - Reason for the proposed absence
    - Arrangements which have been made for the running of the agency during that absence
    - Name, address and qualifications of person responsible for the agency during the absence
    - Arrangements that have been made or are proposed to be made for appointing another person to manage the agency during the absence, including the proposed date by which the appointment is to start [reg.45(2)]
- Where absence arises as a result of an emergency, the registered person must give notice of it within 1 week of its occurrence, specifying the matters mentioned in reg.45(2) (a) to (e) (summarised above) [reg.45(3)].

- Where the registered manager has been absent from the fostering agency for a continuous period of 28 days or more, and the NCSC has not been given notice of the absence, the registered person must without delay give notice in writing to the NCSC specifying the reg.45(2) matters described in bullet points above [reg.45(4)].
- The registered person must notify the NCSC of the return to duty of the registered manager not later than 7 days after the date of her/his return [reg.45 (5)]

Notice of Changes [Reg. 46]

- The registered person must give notice in writing to the NCSC as soon as it is practicable to do so if any of the following events takes place or is proposed to take place:
  - A person other than the registered person carries on or manages the fostering agency
  - A person ceases to carry on or manage the fostering agency
  - Where the registered provider is an individual, s/he changes her/his name
  - Where the registered provider is a partnership, there is any change in the membership of the partnership
  - Where the registered provider is an organisation, its name or address is changed, there is any change of director, manager, secretary or other similar officer of the organisation, there is to be any change in the identity of the responsible individual

- Where the registered provider is an individual, a trustee in bankruptcy is appointed or s/he makes any composition or arrangement with her/his creditors or
- Where the registered provider is a company, or a partnership, a receiver, manager, liquidator or provisional liquidator is appointed in respect of the registered provider [reg.46(1)]

■ The registered provider must notify the NCSC in writing and without delay of the death of the registered manager [reg.46 (2)].

Appointment of Liquidators [Reg. 47]

■ The receiver or manager of the property of a company or partnership which is a registered provider of a fostering agency, a liquidator or provisional liquidator of a company which is the registered provider of a fostering agency or the trustee in bankruptcy of a registered provider of a fostering agency must:

- Immediately notify the NCSC of her/his appointment indicating the reasons for it
- Appoint a manager to take full-time day to day charge of the fostering agency in any case where there is no registered manager and
- Not more than 28 days after appointment notify the NCSC of her/his intentions regarding the future operation of the fostering agency [reg.47(1) and (2)]

Offences [Reg. 48]

- A contravention or failure to comply with any provisions of regulations 3 to 23 and 42 to 46 is an offence [reg. 48(1)].
- NCSC must not bring proceedings against a person in respect of any contravention or failure to comply unless:
  - Notice has been given to her/him in accordance with paragraph reg. 48(3) (below)
  - The period specified in the notice has expired
  - The registered person contravenes or fails to comply with any of the provisions of the regulations mentioned in the notice

NB. NCSC may bring proceedings against a person who was but is no longer a registered person, in respect of failure to comply with regs.22 or 32 [reg.48(4)]

- Where the NCSC considers that the registered person has contravened or failed to comply with any of the provisions of regulations 3 to 23 and 42 to 46, it may serve a notice on the registered person specifying:
  - In what respect in its opinion, the registered person has contravened or is contravening any regulations, or has failed or is failing to comply with requirements of any of the regulations
  - What action, in the opinion of NCSC, the registered person should take so as to comply with any of those regulations, and

- The period, not exceeding 3 months, within which the registered person should take action [reg.48(3)]

Compliance with Regulations [Reg. 49]

- Where there is more than one registered person in respect of an agency, anything required under these regulations to be done by the registered person is, if done by one of the registered persons, not required to be done by any of the other registered persons.

Miscellaneous [Regs. 50 -51]

Transitional Provisions [Reg. 50] & Revocation [Reg.51]

- Time limited provisions are made for those voluntary organisations which place children with foster parents under s.59 (1) CA 1989 and which had made an application for registration before these regulations came into force.
- Reg. 51 confirms revocation of a number of other regulations.

Applications [Regs. 3 – 7 NCSC (Registration) Regulations 2001]

- An application for registration must be:
  - In writing on a form approved by the NCSC
  - Sent or delivered to the NCSC
  - Be accompanied by a recent photograph (which is a true likeness) of the responsible person
  - Give information as described in Reg. 3 (2) –(4) NCSC (Registration) Regulations 2001
- An applicant must supply in writing to the NCSC details of any 'spent' convictions s/he has.
- The responsible person must attend an interview to enable the NCSC to determine whether s/he is fit to carry on or manage the agency [Reg.5 NCSC (Registration) Regulations 2001]
- The applicant must give written notice to the NCSC of any changes after the application is made and before it is determined:
  - Of any change of name or address of applicant or any responsible person
  - Where the applicant is a partnership, of any change of membership of the partnership

- Where applicant is an organisation, any change of director, manager, secretary or other person responsible for organisation's management

- Reg. 7 sets out obligations with respect to information required about staff engaged, after an application is made and before it is determined.

Register & Certificate [Regs. 8, 9 & 10 NCSC (Registration) Regulations 2001]

- The NCSC must maintain a register in respect of fostering agencies and other establishments specified in s.4 (8)(a) and (9)(a) CSA 2000.
- Each register must contain particulars specified in Part 1 and register details in Part 11 Sch. 7 NCSC (Registration) Regulations 2001.
- The contents of a certificate issued by the NCSC will contain particulars specified in Reg.9 NCSC (Registration) Regulations 2001.

NB. *If a person's registration is cancelled, s/he must, not later than the day on which decision / order cancelling it takes effect, return it to the NCSC by delivering / sending it by registered post or recorded delivery [Reg.10]. Failure to comply with Reg.10 is an offence [Reg.11 NCSC (Registration) Regulations 2001].*

Conditions & Reports & Cancellation of Registration [Regs.12 – 15 NCSC (Registration) Regulations 2001]

- Regulation 12 details the process for an application to vary or remove a condition in relation to registration.
- Regulation 13 addresses financial viability and Regulations 14 & 15 specify grounds for cancellation of registration (other grounds for cancellation are contained in s.14 CSA 2000).
- Regulation 15 provides for the registered person to apply for her/his registration to be cancelled.

Registration Fees [Reg. 3 NCSC (Fees & Frequency of Inspections) Regulations 2001]

- Application for registration by a person seeking to be registered as a person who carries on a fostering agency:
  - £1,100-00
- Application for registration by a person seeking to be registered as a person who manages a fostering agency:
  - £300-00

Variation Fees [Reg. 4 NCSC (Fees & Frequency of Inspections) Regulations 2001]

- Application under s.15(1)(a) CSA 2000 – (variation or removal of any condition for time being in force in relation to the registration):
  - £550-00 for registered provider
  - £300-00 for registered manager
- Fee for 'minor variation' (i.e. if successful, not requiring a material alteration to register of NCSC) is £50-00 [reg. 4(4) NCSC (Fees and Frequency of Inspections) Regulations 2001.

Annual Fees [Reg. 5 NCSC (Fees & Frequency of Inspections) Regulations 2001]

- Annual fees for those providing fostering services:
    - Local authority service £1000-00 (due on 01.04.02 for those local authorities running fostering services on 10.01.02 and in all other cases, on the date when they begin to run such services)
    - Fostering agency £1,000-00 (due on 01.04.03 or on the date the certificate is issued, whichever is the later)

Frequency of Inspection [Reg. 6 NCSC (Fees & Frequency of Inspections) Regulations 2001]

- With effect from 01.04.02, the NCSC will inspect both local authority and fostering agencies at a minimum frequency of once in every 12 month period
- Any inspection may be unannounced [Reg. 6 (4) NCSC (Fees & Frequency of Inspections) Regulations 2001].
- A new fostering agency need not be inspected during its first year of operation.

Introduction

- The standards are qualitative, in that they focus on the impact on the individual of the services provided. They are also intended to be measurable and are grouped as follows:
  - Statement of purpose
  - Fitness to carry or manage a fostering service
  - Management of a fostering service
  - Securing and promoting welfare
  - Recruiting, checking, managing, supporting and training staff and foster carers
  - Records
  - Fitness of premises
  - Financial requirements
- Each standard is preceded by a statement of the desired outcome to be achieved by the fostering service provider and the full set of numbered paragraphs of each standard must be met in order to achieve compliance with the standards.
- Regulations to which each standard is linked are cited in the italicised 'outcome' paragraph and unless otherwise specified, refer to the Fostering Services Regulations 2002 and the Children Act 1989 respectively.

Statement of Purpose

Outcome: There is a clear statement of aims and objectives of the fostering service and the service ensures that it meets those aims and objectives [regs. 3 &4].

Standard 1: Statement of Purpose

- **1.1 There is a clear statement of the aims and objectives of the fostering service and of what facilities and services it provides.**
- 1.2 A statement of purpose clearly sets out what services are provided for children who are placed by the fostering service. If education or health services, including therapeutic services are provided, these are covered in the statement of purpose.
- 1.3 The registered provider (for a local authority, the elected members), formally approves the statement of purpose of the fostering service, and reviews, updates and modifies it where necessary and at least annually.
- 1.4 The statement includes details of the fostering service's:
    - Status and constitution (for agencies)
    - Management structure
    - Services
    - Aims, objectives, principles and standards of care
    - Numbers, relevant qualifications and experience of staff

- Numbers of foster carers
- Numbers of children placed
- Numbers of complaints and their outcomes
- Procedures and processes for recruiting, approving, training, supporting and reviewing carers

■ 1.5 The children's guide to the fostering service is suitable for all children fostered through the service, includes a summary of what the service sets out to do for children, and is provided to children as soon as they are fostered, and to all foster carers (if necessary, the guide is produced in different formats to meet the needs of different groups of children). The children's guide contains information on how a child can secure access to an independent advocate and about how to complain.

■ 1.6 The fostering service's policies, procedures and any written guidance to staff and carers accurately reflect the statement of purpose.

Fitness to provide or manage a fostering service

Outcome: The fostering service is provided and managed by those with the appropriate skills and experience to do so efficiently and effectively and by those who are suitable to work with children [regs 5, 7 – 8 & 10].

Standard 2: Skills to Carry on or Manage

- **2.1 The people involved in carrying on and managing the fostering service possess the necessary business and management skills and financial expertise to manage the work efficiently and effectively and have the necessary knowledge and experience of child care and fostering to do so in a professional manner.**
- 2.2 The manager has:
  - A professional qualification relevant to working with children, which must be either NVQ level 4 or the Dip SW or another qualification that matches the competencies required by the NVQ Level 4
  - By 2005, a qualification at level 4 NVQ in management or another qualification which matches the competencies required by the NVQ Level 4; and
  - At least two years' experience of working with children within the past five years, and in addition at least one year's experience of working at a senior level

- 2.3 For the transitional period in relation to management qualifications, appointees to the post of manager who have no such qualifications begin appropriate management training within six months of appointment.
- 2.4 The manager exercises effective leadership of the staff and operation, such that the fostering service is organised, managed and staffed in a manner that delivers the best possible child care.

Standard 3: Suitability To Carry On or Manage

- **3.1 Any persons carrying on or managing the fostering service are suitable people to run a business concerned with safeguarding and promoting the welfare of children.**
- 3.2 For the references set out in Schedule 1 of the Fostering Services Regulations 2002, telephone enquiries are made to follow up written references.
- 3.3 Police checks are renewed every three years.
- 3.4 Records are kept of checks and references that have been obtained and their outcomes.

Management of the fostering service

Outcome: The fostering service is managed ethically and efficiently, delivering a good quality foster care service and avoiding confusion and conflicts of role [regs 5 – 8, 10, 20 & 4].

Standard 4: Monitoring & Controlling

- **4.1 There are clear procedures for monitoring and controlling the activities of the fostering service and ensuring quality performance.**
- 4.2 There are clear roles for managers and staff and well established lines of communication and of accountability between managers, staff and carers.
- 4.3 The service has proper financial procedures and there is a reviewing procedure to keep them up to date.
- 4.4 Information is provided to purchasers of services and others including:
  - Charges for each of its services
  - Statements of amounts paid to foster carers, and
  - Itemised amounts paid for wider services which may include health and education
- 4.5 The fostering service informs carers, managers and staff of their responsibility to declare any possible conflicts of interest.

Standard 5: Managing Effectively & Efficiently

- **5.1 The fostering service is managed effectively and efficiently.**
- 5.2 The manager has a clear job description setting out duties and responsibilities and does not hold a similar position in another organisation.
- 5.3 The level of delegation and responsibility of the manager, and the lines of accountability, are clearly defined.
- 5.4 Clear arrangements are in place to identify the person in charge when the manager is absent.

Securing and promoting welfare

Outcome: The fostering service promotes and safeguards the child/young person's physical, mental and emotional welfare [regs 11- 16 & 18].

Standard 6: Providing Suitable Foster Carers

- **6.1 The fostering service makes available foster carers who provide a safe, healthy and nurturing environment.**
- 6.2 The foster home can comfortably accommodate all who live there and is inspected annually to make sure that it meets the needs of foster children.
- 6.3 The home is warm, adequately furnished and decorated and is maintained to a good standard of cleanliness and hygiene.
- 6.4 Each child placed has her/his own bed and accommodation arrangements reflect the child's assessed need for privacy and space or for any specific need resulting from a disability.
- 6.5 If the child has been abused or has abused another child, then the child's needs and the needs of all other children in the home are assessed before any decision is made to allow sharing of bedrooms. The outcome of that assessment is recorded in writing.

- 6.6 The home and immediate environment are free of avoidable hazards that might expose a child to risk of injury or harm and contain safety barriers and equipment appropriate to the child's age, development and level of ability.
- 6.7 The foster carer's preparation and training cover health and safety issues and the carer is provided with written guidelines on their health and safety responsibilities.
- 6.8 Where the foster carer is expected to provide transport for the child, the fostering service ensures this is safe and appropriate to the child's needs.
- 6.9 Foster carers understand that they may be interviewed or visited as part of the Commission's inspection process.

Standard 7: Valuing Diversity

- **7.1 The fostering service ensures children and young people, and their families, are provided with foster care services which value diversity and promote equality.**
- 7.2 Each child and family have access to foster care services which recognise and address needs in terms of gender, religion, ethnic origin, language, culture, disability and sexuality. If a foster placement has to be made in an emergency and no suitable placement is available in terms of the above, then steps are taken to achieve the above within 6 weeks.
- 7.3 The fostering service ensures foster carers and social workers work co-operatively to enhance the child's confidence and feeling of self-worth and carers' and social workers' training covers this issue.
- 7.4 Fostering service ensures that their foster carers provide care which respects and preserves each child's ethnic, religious, cultural and linguistic background and foster carers' preparation and training cover this.
- 7.5 The fostering service ensures their foster carers support and encourage each child to develop skills to help her/him to deal with all forms of discrimination and foster carers' preparation and training cover this.
- 7.6 Each child with a disability receives specific services and support to help her/him to maximise potential and lead as full a life as possible, including appropriate

equipment and, where necessary and appropriate, adaptation of the carer's home and/or vehicle.

- 7.7 The fostering service ensures that their foster carers give each child encouragement and equal access to opportunities to develop and pursue her/his talents, interests and hobbies. This is set out in the information provided to foster carers. Disabled children are provided with services and supports which enable them to access as wide a range of activities as is possible for them.

Standard 8: Matching

- **8.1 Local authority fostering services, and voluntary agencies placing children in their own right, ensure that each child or young person placed in foster care is carefully matched with a carer capable of meeting her/his assessed needs. For agencies providing foster carers to local authorities, those agencies ensure that they offer carers only if they represent appropriate matches for a child for whom a local authority is seeking a carer.**

- 8.2 In matching children with carers, responsible authorities take into account the child's care plan and recent written assessments of the child and their family and the carers.

- 8.3 Matches are achieved by means of information sharing and consideration involving all relevant professionals, the child and her/his family and potential carers, their families and other children in placement.

- 8.4 Written foster placement agreements contain specific reference to elements of matching which were taken into consideration in agreeing the placement and identify areas where foster carers need additional support to compensate for any gaps in the match between the child and carer.

- 8.5 Placement decisions consider the child's assessed racial, ethnic, religious, cultural and linguistic needs and match these as closely as possible with the ethnic origin, race, religion, culture and language of the foster family.

- 8.6 Where transracial or transcommunity placements are made, the responsible authority provides the foster family with additional training, support and information to enable the child to be provided with the best possible care and to develop a positive understanding of her/his heritage.
- 8.7 Where practicable, each child has the opportunity for a period of introduction to a proposed foster carer so she/he can express an informed view about the placement and become familiar with the carer, the carer's family, any other children in placement, and the home, neighbourhood and any family pets, before moving in. Information for carers explains that this approach is used when possible.

Standard 9: Protecting From Abuse & Neglect

- **9.1 The fostering service protects each child or young person from all forms of abuse, neglect, exploitation and deprivation.**
- 9.2 Training for foster carers includes training in caring for a child who has been abused, safe caring skills, managing behaviour and recognising signs of abuse and ways of boosting and maintaining child's self-esteem.
- 9.3 Safe caring guidelines are provided, based on a written policy, for each foster home, in consultation with the carer and everyone else in the household. The guidelines are cleared with the child's social worker and are explained clearly and appropriately to the child.
- 9.4 The fostering service makes clear to the foster carers that corporal punishment is not acceptable and that this includes smacking, slapping, shaking and all other humiliating forms of treatment or punishment. This is set out clearly in written information for foster carers.
- 9.5 Management systems are in place to collate and evaluate information on the circumstances, number and outcome of all allegations of neglect or abuse of a child in foster care. The information is scrutinised regularly.
- 9.6 The fostering service ensures foster carers are aware of the particular vulnerability of looked after children and their susceptibility to bullying and procedures are in

place to recognise, record and address any instance of bullying and to help foster carers cope with it.

- 9.7 Each foster carer is provided with full information about the foster child and her/his family to enable the carer to protect the foster child, their own children, other children for whom they have responsibility and themselves.
- 9.8 The fostering service makes sure that the foster carer has a clear written procedure for use if the foster child is missing from home.

Standard 10: Promoting Contact

- **10.1 The fostering service makes sure that each child or young person in foster care is encouraged to maintain and develop family contacts and friendships as set out in her/his care plan and/or foster placement agreement.**
- 10.2 There are clear procedures setting out how appropriate contact arrangements for each child in foster care are to be established, maintained, monitored and reviewed.
- 10.3 The fostering service considers the need for and benefits of appropriate contact for the child when finding/suggesting a suitable foster carer. Attention is paid to supporting contact where the child is placed outside of the area.
- 10.4 The views of the child or young person are sought and given weight in determining contact arrangements.
- 10.5 In assessment and training of carers, the fostering service stresses the importance of foster carers helping a child to maintain appropriate contacts and covers the skills required to encourage and facilitate such contacts.
- 10.6 Except where an overriding requirement exists, eg a court order, the fostering service ensures that contact does not take place until the child's social worker has carried out a risk assessment and arrangements made for any supervision that is needed.

- 10.7 The fostering service provides help and support to the carer in dealing with any difficult contact issues that may arise. The fostering service provider ensures that the role of the foster carer in supporting contact arrangements, including any arrangements for the supervision of contact are clearly articulated in the Foster Placement Agreement.
- 10.8 Financial support is provided to the carer for transport or other costs involved in ensuring contacts take place at the desired frequency and in the most suitable place.
- 10.9 The fostering service ensures that the carer records outcomes of contact arrangements and their perceived impact on the child; this information is fed back to the child's social worker.

Standard 11: Consultation

- **11.1 The fostering service ensures that children's opinions, and those of their families and others significant to the child, are sought over all issues likely to affect their daily life and future.**
- 11.2 The fostering service ensures that all foster carers understand the importance of listening to the views of the children in their care, and are trained and supported in listening and responding to children's views.
- 11.3 The fostering service ensures that the opinions and views of children on all matters affecting them, including day-to-day matters, are ascertained on a regular and frequent basis and not taken for granted.
- 11.4 Suitable means are provided, frequently, for any child with communication difficulties to make their wishes and feelings known regarding their care and treatment.
- 11.5 The fostering service ensures that children in foster care know how to raise any concerns or complaints, and ensures that they receive prompt feedback on any concerns or complaints raised.

Standard 12: Promoting Development & Health

- **12.1 The fostering service ensures that it provides foster care services which help each child or young person in foster care to receive health care which meets her/his needs for physical, emotional and social development, together with information and training appropriate to her/his age and understanding to enable informed participation in decisions about her/his health needs.**

- 12.2 The fostering service is informed about health services, including specialist services, available in the area it covers and takes this into account when finding/suggesting a foster carer for a child. The fostering service ensures that no placement is made which prevents a child from continuing to receive the specialist health care services they need.

- 12.3 Before a placement begins, the carer is provided with as full a description as possible of the health needs of a child and clear procedures governing consent for the child to receive medical treatment. Where there is an agency placement, the responsible authority provides this information to the agency and the agency passes it on to the carer. If full details of the health needs are not available before placement, a high priority is given to ensuring that the information is obtained and passed to the foster carer once the placement is made.

- 12.4 The carer is provided with a written health record for each child placed in their care; this is updated during the placement and moves with the child. Depending upon age and understanding, child has access to and understands health record kept by the fostering service.
- 12.5 Each carer is given basic training on health and hygiene issues and first aid, with particular emphasis on health promotion and communicable diseases.
- 12.6 The fostering service makes clear to the carer their role in terms of helping to promote the health of any child in their care, including:
    - Registering a child with a doctor or dentist when necessary
    - Taking the child to any health appointments, including dental and optician appointments, when required
    - Helping her/him to access the services that she/he needs
    - Giving attention to health issues in everyday care of the child, including diet, personal hygiene, health promotion issues etc
    - Acting as an advocate on the child's behalf
- 12.7 The fostering service has good links with health agencies and helps the carer to secure services for the child when necessary.
- 12.8 The fostering service requires foster carers to supply information about the child's health needs for the planning and review process.

Standard 13: Promoting Educational Achievement

- **13.1 The fostering service gives a high priority to meeting the educational needs of each child or young person in foster care and ensures that she/he is encouraged to attain her/his full potential**
- 13.2 The fostering service gives high priority to helping their foster carers to meet a child's education needs.
- 13.3 The fostering service requires foster carers to contribute to the assessment of the child's educational needs and progress for the planning and review process. The fostering service helps the foster carer to contribute to the delivery of any personal education plan.
- 13.4 The foster carer's role in school contact, e.g., parents evenings, open days, discussions with teachers, in conjunction with the birth parent where appropriate and in line with the care plan, is clearly laid out in the placement agreement.
- 13.5 The fostering service ensures that their foster carers provide an environment in which education and learning are valued; and that the foster carer establishes an expectation of regular attendance at school, and supports the child's full participation through provision of necessary uniform and equipment, support for completion of homework, and financial and other support for attending school trips and after school activities.

- 13.6 The fostering service has information systems to demonstrate the educational attainment of the children and young people in their foster care services and to demonstrate the numbers excluded from school.
- 13.7 The fostering service makes clear its expectations (in relation to school-day responsibilities) of foster carers and the arrangements which will be put in place if any child in their care is not in school. Those arrangements include structured occupation during school hours.
- 13.8 The foster placement agreement identifies where financial responsibility lies for all school costs, including school uniform, school trips and school equipment.

Standard 14: Preparing For Adulthood

- **14.1 The fostering service ensures that their foster care services help to develop skills, competence and knowledge necessary for adult living.**
- 14.2 There are clear written requirements of what is expected of foster carers in terms of preparing children and young people for independent or semi-independent living.
- 14.3 Foster carers receive training and support to enable them to provide effective support and guidance to a young person preparing to move into independent or semi-independent living.
- 14.4 The fostering service ensures that foster carers understand that they need to provide all children in their care with age and developmentally appropriate opportunities for learning independence skills.
- 14.5 The fostering service ensures that each young person preparing to move to independent or semi-independent living is consulted about her/his future and encouraged to be actively involved in decision making processes and implementation of the Pathway Plan.

Recruiting, checking, managing, supporting and training staff and foster carers

Outcome: The people who work in or for the fostering service are suitable to work with children and young people and they are managed, trained and supported in such a way as to ensure the best possible outcomes for children in foster care. The number of staff and carers and their range of qualifications and experience are sufficient to achieve the purposes and functions of the organisation [regs 17, 19 - 21 & 27 - 28].

Standard 15: Suitability To Work with Children

- **15.1 Any people working in or for the fostering service are suitable to work with children and young people and to safeguard and promote their welfare.**
- 15.2 There are clear written recruitment and selection procedures for appointing staff which follow good practice in safeguarding children and young people. All personnel responsible for recruitment and selection of staff are trained in, understand and operate these.
- 15.3 All people working in or for the fostering service are interviewed as part of the selection process and have references checked to assess suitability before taking on responsibilities. Telephone enquiries are made as well as obtaining written references.

- 15.4 Records are kept of checks and references that have been obtained and their outcomes. Police checks are renewed every three years.

- 15.5 All social work staff have an appropriate qualification, or are in the course of obtaining a suitable professional qualification, to work with children and young people, their families and foster carers, and have a good understanding of foster care. They have appropriate knowledge and skills, including:
  - Understanding of the Children Act, the Children Act regulations and guidance,
  - Relevant current policies and procedures, Working Together and associated child protection guidance, the Framework for the Assessment of Children in Need and their Families, the regulatory requirements under the Care Standards Act 2000 and adoption law
  - Knowledge of the growth and development of children and an ability to communicate with children and young people
  - Understanding the importance of a complaints procedure
  - An ability to promote equality, diversity and the rights of individuals and groups
  - Knowledge of the roles of other agencies, in particular health and education.

- 15.6 Any social work staff involved in assessment and approval of foster carers are qualified social workers, have experience of foster care and family placement work and are trained in assessment. Students and others who do not meet this requirement carry out assessments and approvals under the supervision of someone who does, who takes responsibility for the assessments and approvals.

- 15.7 All educationalists, psychologists, therapists and other professional staff are professionally qualified and appropriately trained to work with children and young people, their families and foster carers, and have a good understanding of foster care.
- 15.8 Where unqualified staff carry out social work functions they do so under the direct supervision of qualified social workers, who are accountable for their work.

Standard 16: Organisation & Management of Staff

- **16.1 Staff are organised and managed in a way which delivers an efficient and effective foster care service.**
- 16.2 There is a clear management structure with clear lines of accountability.
- 16.3 Staff are managed and monitored by people who have appropriate skills and qualifications.
- 16.4 The level of management delegation and responsibility are clearly defined and are appropriate for the skills, qualifications and experience of relevant members of staff.
- 16.5 The fostering service has systems in place to determine, prioritise and monitor workloads and assign tasks to appropriate staff.
- 16.6 There are structures and systems in place to ensure carer assessments, approvals and reviews are managed and implemented effectively. Local authorities using agencies check the NCSC inspection reports before doing so, to ensure that there are no concerns about the agencies' assessment, approval and review processes.
- 16.7 Where a local authority fostering service uses an agency to provide a foster carer, they have a system to ensure that the quality of care to be provided is clearly specified in the contract and appropriate monitoring arrangements are in place to ensure compliance.

- 16.8 Professional supervision and consultation are provided for social work staff by appropriately qualified and experienced staff.
- 16.9 Staff and carers undertake on-going training and appropriate professional and skills development. Carers maintain a training portfolio.
- 16.10 There is adequate administrative back up, office equipment, and infrastructure to enable staff who recruit, assess, supervise, support and train foster carers to carry out their duties in an efficient and effective manner.
- 16.11 There is an appropriate level of clerical and administrative support.
- 16.12 Administrative procedures are appropriate for dealing promptly with enquiries from prospective carers and any new request for services.
- 16.13 There is access to the range of advice needed to provide a full service for children and young people and to support carers. This includes appropriate childcare, medical, educational and other professional and legal advice.
- 16.14 All employees, sessional workers and consultants are provided with appropriate written contracts, job descriptions and conditions of service.
- 16.15 All fostering service social workers understand the role of the children's social workers, and there is a clear understanding about how the fostering service social workers and the children's social workers work effectively together.

- 16.16 Staff have a copy of:
  - Policies and working practices in respect of grievances and disciplinary matters
  - Details of the services offered
  - The equal opportunities policy
  - Health and safety procedures

Standard 17: Sufficient Staff / Carers with Right Skills / Experience

- **17.1 The fostering service has an adequate number of sufficiently experienced and qualified staff and recruits a range of carers to meet needs of children and young people for whom it aims to provide a service.**
- 17.2 The full time equivalent staffing complement, in terms of numbers, grades, experience and qualifications, is adequate to meet, at all times, needs of the service and is line with the statement of purpose.
- 17.3 Where a shortfall in staffing levels occurs, there are contingency plans to resolve the situation.
- 17.4 Staff policies encourage retention of salaried staff – including training, regular supervision, study leave, clear workloads and terms and conditions – and of carers by providing support, training and services.
- 17.5 The service has a recruitment policy and strategy aimed at recruiting a range of carers to meet needs of children for whom it aims to provide a service.
- 17.6 There is a clearly set out assessment process for carers which defines the:
  - Task to be undertaken
  - Qualities, competences or aptitudes being sought or to be achieved

- Standards to be applied in the assessment
- Stages and content of the selection process and the timescales involved
- Information to be given to applicants

■ 17.7 In assessing qualities, competences and aptitudes, services consider them in relation to:

- Child rearing
- Caring for children born to somebody else
- Contact between fostered children and their families
- Helping children make sense of their past
- Sexual boundaries and attitudes
- Awareness of issues around child abuse
- Approaches to discipline
- Awareness of how to promote secure attachments between children and appropriate adults
- Awareness of own motivation for fostering / own needs to be met through the fostering process
- Religion and racial / cultural / linguistic issues
- Standard of living and lifestyle
- Health
- Own experience of parenting and being parented
- Own experiences in relation to disability and/or attitudes to disability

Standard 18: Fair & Competent Employer

- **18.1 The fostering service is a fair and competent employer, with sound employment practices and good support for its staff and carers.**
- 18.2 There are sound employment practices, in relation to both staff and carers.
- 18.3 Out of hours management and support services are available for foster carers.
- 18.4 There are management systems for carer supervision, appraisal and support.
- 18.5 There is a comprehensive health and safety policy for carers, children and staff which covers all legal requirements.
- 18.6 For agencies, there is a public liability and professional indemnity insurance for all staff and carers. The insurance policy covers costs arising as a result of child abuse claims against any staff or carers.
- 18.7 There is a whistleblowing policy which is made known to all staff and carers.

Standard 19: Training

- **19.1 There is a good quality training programme to enhance individual skills and to keep staff up-to-date with professional and legal developments.**
- 19.2 There is a clear plan for the training and development of all staff involved in fostering work through induction, post-qualifying and in-service training. All new staff are given induction training commencing within 7 days of starting their employment and being completed within 10 weeks.
- 19.3 There is an appraisal or joint review scheme which identifies the training and development needs of all staff involved in fostering work and carers. Individual programmes of training are available, outcomes are monitored and linked to assessment of staff and carer needs, and relate to the tasks assigned to them.
- 19.4 All employees are kept informed of changes in any legislation or guidance that are relevant to their jobs.
- 19.5 The effectiveness of training programmes for the staff providing the fostering service is routinely evaluated and training programmes are reviewed and updated at least annually.
- 19.6 Training programmes reflect the policies of the fostering service.
- 19.7 Joint training between fostering service staff and foster carers is held on a regular basis.

Standard 20: Accountability & Support

- **20.1 All staff are properly accountable and supported.**
- 20.2 All staff have clear written details of the duties and responsibilities expected of them, together with the policies and procedures of the organisation.
- 20.3 All staff who come into contact with foster carers and prospective foster carers and children/young people receive management supervision and a record is kept by the line manager of the content of the supervision and of progress made. Supervision sessions are regular and planned in advance.
- 20.4 Staff receive regular, planned appraisals from their line manager.
- 20.5 Each member of staff has the opportunity to attend regular staff and team meetings.

Standard 21: Management & Support of Carers

- **21.1 The fostering service has a clear strategy for working with and supporting carers.**
- 21.2 There is a clear strategy for working with carers that is documented and understood. This includes:
  - Arrangements for training and development
  - Encouragement for self help groups
  - Supervision
  - Support services
  - Information and advice
  - Assistance in dealing with other relevant services, such as health and education
  - Out-of-hours support
  - Respite care
  - Arrangements for reviews.

NB. There are no standards 21.3 and 21.4

- 21.5 The role of the supervising social worker is clear both to the worker and the carer. Annual review reports are prepared and are available to the Fostering Panel.
- 21.6 There is a good system of communication between the fostering service social workers and the child's social worker.

Standard 22: Supervision of Carers

- **22. 1 The fostering service is a managed one which provides supervision for foster carers and helps them to develop their skills.**
- 22.2 Foster care agreements ensure foster carers have a full understanding of what is expected of foster carers, the agency and/or the local authority.
- 22.3 Each approved foster carer is supervised by a named, appropriately qualified social worker and has access to adequate social work and other professional support, information and advice to enable her or him to provide consistent, high quality care for a child or young person placed in her or his home. The supervising social worker ensures each carer she or he supervises is informed in writing of, and accepts, understands and operates within, all standards, policies and guidance agreed by the fostering service.
- 22.4 In producing the Foster Care Agreement for a foster carer, in line with Schedule 5 of the Fostering Services Regulations 2002, the fostering provider ensures that the Agreement contains the information they need to know, in a comprehensible style, to carry out their functions as a foster carer effectively.
- 22.5 On approval, carers are given a handbook which covers policies, procedures, guidance, legal information and insurance details. This is updated regularly.

- 22.6 Supervising social workers meet regularly with foster carers. Meetings have a clear purpose and provide the opportunity to supervise the foster carers' work. Foster carers' files include records of supervisory meetings. There are occasional unannounced visits, at least one each year.

- 22.7 There is a system of practical support for carers, including:
    - Out of hours management support
    - Prompt payment
    - Insurance cover
    - Support for foster care associations
    - Respite care where appropriate
    - Access to social work support

- 22.8 Information about the procedures for dealing with complaints and representations is widely available. Complaints and representations are recorded and monitored and the outcome evaluated to inform future provision of services.

- 22.9 Information about the procedures to deal with investigations into allegations is made known to foster care staff, carers and children and young people and includes the provision of independent support to the foster carer/s during an investigation.

- 22.10 Records about allegations of abuse are kept and monitored and there is a clear policy framework which outlines the circumstances in which a carer should be removed from the foster carer register.

Standard 23: Training of Carers

- **23.1 The fostering service ensures that foster carers are trained in the skills required to provide high quality care and meet the needs of each child/young person placed in their care.**
- 23.2 Pre-approval and induction training for each carer includes opportunities to benefit from the experience and knowledge of existing carers. All new foster carers receive induction training.
- 23.3 All training fits within a framework of equal opportunities, anti-discriminatory practice and is organised to encourage and facilitate attendance by foster carers, for example by including convenient times and venues and by providing childcare and reasonable expenses.
- 23.4 Where two adults in one household are approved as joint carers, both successfully complete all training. Each foster carer is trained in identified key areas prior to any child being placed in his or her home. Attention is given to the training needs of particular groups, eg male carers.
- 23.5 There is an on-going programme of training and self-development for foster carers to develop their skills and tackle any weaknesses.
- 23.6 Appropriate training on safe caring is provided for all members of the foster household.

- 23.7 Specific consideration is given to any help or support needed by the sons and daughters of foster carers.
- 23.8 Each carer's Annual Review includes an appraisal of training and development needs, which is documented in the review report.
- 23.9 The effectiveness of training received is evaluated and reviewed annually.

Records

Local authority fostering services may maintain some records within the part of the department responsible for supervising the child's placement, rather than the fostering services. Nothing in these standards requires two separate parts of the department to maintain duplicate sets of records, as long as both parts have access to the records.

Outcome: All appropriate records are kept and are accessible in relation to the fostering services and the individual foster carers and foster children [regs 22 & 30].

Standard 24: Case Records For Children

- **24.1 The fostering service ensures that an up-to-date, comprehensive case record is maintained for each child or young person in foster care which details the nature and quality of care provided and contributes to an understanding of her/his life events. Relevant information from the case records is made available to the child and to anyone involved in her/his care.**
- 24.2 There is a written policy on case recording which establishes the purpose, format and contents of files, and clarifies what information is kept on the foster carer's files and what information is kept on the child's files.
- 24.3 Where there is an agency placement the agency works with the responsible authority to ensure effective integration of information held in the agency's case files and those of the responsible authority.

The agency provides copies of the records and documents in relation to children placed by a responsible authority immediately, on receipt of a written request. When a child leaves an agency foster care placement, the agency sends all relevant records to the responsible authority.

- 24.4 The fostering service ensures that the foster carer knows why the child is in foster care and understands the basis for the current placement, its intended duration and purpose, and the details of the child's legal status.

- 24.5 The foster carer encourages the child to reflect on and understand her/his history, according to the child's age and ability, and to keep appropriate memorabilia. The fostering service makes this role clear to their foster carers.

- 24.6 The fostering service gives the foster carer access to all relevant information to help the child understand and come to terms with past events. (Where necessary information is not forthcoming from the responsible authority, a copy of the written request for information is kept.)

- 24.7 The carer is trained and provided with the necessary equipment to record significant life events for the child, and to encourage the child to make such recordings, including photograph albums.

- 24.8 The fostering service ensures that their carers store information in a secure manner and understand what information they are expected to keep and what information needs to be passed on to the fostering service.

Standard 25: Administrative Records

- **25.1 The fostering service's administrative records contain all significant information relevant to the running of the service and as required by regulations.**
- 25.2 Separate records are kept for:
  - Staff, employed and independent / sessional
  - Carers
  - Children
  - complaints
  - Allegations
- 25.3 There is a system to monitor quality and adequacy of records, and remedial action is taken when necessary.
- 25.4 Confidential records are stored securely at all times and there is a clear policy on access.
- 25.5 Records are in a form which can be readily passed on if a child moves to another placement or ceases to be looked after or if references are requested on staff or carer.
- 25.6 There is a permanent, private, secure record for each child and foster carer referred to or appointed by the organisation. This can, in compliance with legal requirements for safeguards, be seen by the child and by her/his parents or foster carers.

- 25.7 There is a written policy and procedural guidance for staff for keeping and retention of case files ensuring foster carers, fostered children and their parents know the nature of records maintained and how to access them.
- 25.8 There is a procedure on storing and managing confidential information that is known to panel members, staff and specialist advisers.
- 25.9 Written entries in records are legible, clearly expressed, non-stigmatising, and distinguish between fact, opinion and third party information.
- 25.10 The system for keeping records is congruent with the Looking After Children System / Integrated Children's System.
- 25.11 Records are kept of checks and references that have been obtained and their outcomes.
- 25.12 Children and foster carers are encouraged to access their records, make additions and comments and record personal statements, including any dissent.
- 25.13 There is a system for keeping records about allegations and complaints and for handling these confidentially and securely. Records of complaints and allegations are clearly recorded on the relevant files for staff, carers and children – including details of the investigation, conclusion reached and action taken. Separate records are also kept which bring together data on allegations and on complaints.

Fitness of premises for use as fostering service

Outcome: The premises used as offices by the fostering provider are suitable for the purpose [reg. 23].

Standard 26: Premises

- **26.1 Premises used as offices by the fostering service are appropriate for the purpose.**
- 26.2 There are identifiable office premises to which staff and others with a legitimate interest have access during normal office hours.
- 26.3 There are efficient and robust administrative systems, including IT and communication systems. Premises have:
  - Facilities for the secure retention of records in a lockable room
  - Appropriate measures to safeguard IT systems and
  - An appropriate security system
- 26.4 Premises provide an equipped base from which staff work.
- 26.5 The premises and its contents are adequately insured (or there are alternative prompt methods of replacing lost items).

Section 8 Financial requirements

Outcome: The agency fostering services are financially viable and appropriate and timely payments are made to foster carers [reg. 44].

Standard 27: Financial Viability

- **27.1 The agency ensures it is financially viable at all times and has sufficient financial resources to fulfil its obligations.**
- 27.2 Procedures exist to deal with situations of financial crisis, such as disclosing information to purchasers and liaising with them to safeguard the welfare of children receiving services through the agency.
- 27.3 Regulations and guidelines imposed upon businesses are conformed with, including Income Tax (PAYE), National Insurance and VAT.

Standard 28: Financial Processes

- **28.1 The financial processes / systems of the agency are properly operated and maintained in accordance with sound and appropriate accounting standards and practice.**
- 28.2 The agency has clearly documented financial arrangements for control and supervision of its financial affairs and powers.

- 28.3 The agency has a clearly written set of principles and standards governing its financial management and these are communicated to its managers and accountants.
- 28.4 The agency has a written set of principles describing financial procedures and responsibilities to be followed by all staff, consultants, professional experts, directors, trustees and any manager.
- 28.5 Accounts are maintained and properly audited by a registered accountant.
- 28.6 The registered provider regularly receives information on the financial state of the agency.
- 28.7 The agency publishes its charges for each of its services and has a clear policy for charging of fees and expenses for any additional services it is asked to provide (all available on request to purchasers and others with a legitimate interest).

Standard 29: Payment to Carers

- **29.1 Each carer receives an allowance and agreed expenses covering full cost of caring for each child placed. Payments are made promptly at the agreed time and allowances and fees are reviewed annually.**
- 29.2 There is a written policy on fostering allowances. This and the current allowance levels are well publicised and provided annually to each carer. The carer receives clear information about the allowances and expenses payable and how to access them, before a child is placed.

Fostering panels

Outcome:: Fostering panels are organised efficiently and effectively so as to ensure that good quality decisions are made about the approval of foster carers, in line with the overriding objective to promote and safeguard the welfare of children in foster care [regs 24 - 26].

Standard 30: Fostering Panels

- **30.1 Fostering panels have clear written policies and procedures, which are implemented in practice, about the handling of their functions.**
- 30.2 The written procedures cover decision-making when all members of the panel are not in agreement.
- 30.3 There are requirements about suitability of foster panel members, including Criminal Record Bureau checks. No panel members are allowed to begin work until all checks have been satisfactorily completed.
- 30.4 Fostering panels have access to medical expertise as required.
- 30.5 Fostering panels provide a quality assurance function in relation to the assessment process – in particular to monitor and review the work of the assessors; to provide feedback; to identify problems; and to ensure that there is consistency of approach in assessment across the service, that it is fair to all applicants and that it has been completed in a thorough and rigorous way.

- 30.6 Foster panels receive management information about the outcome of foster carers' annual reviews.
- 30.7 For local authority panels, the panel monitors the range and type of carers available to the authority in comparison with the needs of children.
- 30.8 The independent members of the panel include, as far as possible, expertise in education and in child health.
- 30.9 One of the independent members is normally a person who has at any time been placed with foster carers or whose child has at any time been placed with foster carers.

Short-term breaks

Outcome: When foster care is provided as a short-term break for a child, the arrangements recognise that the parents remain the main carers for the child.

Standard 31: Short-Term Breaks

- **31.1 Where a fostering service provides short-term breaks for children in foster care, they have policies and procedures, implemented in practice, to meet the particular needs of children receiving short-term breaks.**
- 31.2 Where appropriate, requirements for foster care placements for short-term breaks are different from those for children being fostered for longer periods. In particular, birth parents remain central to the promotion of health and education needs.

Family and friends as carers

Outcome: Local authority fostering services' policies and procedures for assessing, approving, supporting and training foster carers recognise the particular contribution that can be made by, and the particular needs of family and friends as carers.

Standard 32: Family & Friends As Carers

- **32.1 These standards are all relevant to carers who are family and friends of the child, but there is a recognition of the particular relationship and position of family and friends carers.**
- 32.2 Local authority fostering services are sensitive to pre-existing relationships in assessing and approving family and friends as foster carers.
- 32.3 The support and training needs for family and friends carers are assessed and met in the same way as for any other carers.
- 32.4 The mechanisms within a local authority fostering service for assessing and approving family and friend carers are designed in a way that encourages their consideration as carers.

Appendix 1: Source Documents

- Care Standards Act 2000
- Children Act 1989
- Fostering Services Regulations 2002
- Children Act (Miscellaneous Amendments) (England) Regulations 2002
- National Care Standards Commission (Registration) Regulations 2001
- National Care Standards Commission (Fees and Frequency of Inspections) Regulations 2001
- National Minimum Standards
- UK National Standards for Foster Care NFCA 1999
- Code of Practice on the recruitment, assessment, approval, training, managements and support of foster carers NFCA 1999

Appendix 2: CAE Publications

- **Personal Guides:**
  - Children Act 1989 in the Context of the Human Rights Act 1998
  - Childminding and Day Care (England)
  - Child Protection
  - Residential Care of Children
  - Fostering
  - How Old Do I Have To Be…? (a simple guide to the rights and responsibilities of 0 - 21 year olds)
  - Adoption Act 1976
  - Domestic Violence (Part IV Family Law Act 1996 & Protection from Harassment Act 1997)
  - Human Fertilisation and Embryology Act 1990
  - Looking After Children: Good Parenting, Good Outcomes (DH LAC System)
  - Crime and Disorder Act 1998 in the Context of The Powers of Criminal Courts (Sentencing) Act 2000

  (Discounts for orders of 100 or more of any one title)

- All available from:

  Children Act Enterprises Ltd 103 Mayfield Road South Croydon Surrey CR2 0BH tel: 020 8651 0554 fax: 020 8405 8483 e-mail: childact@dial.pipex.com

  www.caeuk.org